Praise for *Powerful (*

By applying sound educational theory to curriculum practice, Powerful Geography does precisely what the teaching profession needs more of. Drawing on a range of educational ideas, old and new, Mark Enser takes the reader beyond the traditional–progressive divide to explore questions of the purpose of geography education, different approaches to teaching the subject, how to sequence a curriculum, how to select places to study, and how to respond to calls for the curriculum to be driven by political objectives. In doing so, he brings the disciplinary focus back into the geography curriculum and shows teachers how to nurture geographical thinking in their students.

Alex Standish, Associate Professor of Geography Education, UCL Institute of Education

Powerful Geography powerfully offers geography curriculum leaders and teachers the opportunity to reflect on key curriculum questions and the means to navigate existing geography education scholarship. The curation of contributions from both primary and secondary teachers woven in as case studies perfectly illustrates why thinking deeply and engaging with subject community discourse is vital for empowering teachers in their professional learning and teaching.

Grace Healy, Curriculum Director, David Ross Education Trust

In *Powerful Geography*, Mark takes us on a journey towards greater clarity about what it means to truly teach this multidisciplinary subject with purpose. As we take this journey with Mark, he provides a convincing evidence-based argument about why geography teachers should take time to reflect on the purpose of their geography curriculum so that it shifts from "anything is geography" to a curriculum that builds the foundations for Future 3, which is a focus on a deeper understanding of our ever-changing world. Along with the reasons for change, Mark provides a wealth of strategies to teach geography with purpose – and the case studies provide a glimpse through the keyhole of these discussions in practice. I highly recommend this book to all geography teachers.

Michael Chiles, Geography Trust Lead, The King's Leadership Academy, and author of *The Feedback Pendulum*

Powerful Geography is an enjoyable read. It walks you through some relevant, philosophical and theoretical thinking underpinning curriculum development in accessible and engaging ways. Although the book predominantly draws on examples from the secondary phase of education, there is much that is relevant for primary practitioners too.

It is also about empowering teachers: as curriculum-makers, thinkers, subject experts and, most of all, as teachers who can offer the gift of teaching. The value of signature pedagogies such as enquiry and fieldwork are set out with clear rationales as to how they might be purposefully planned for and enacted within a coherent curriculum. Mark identifies some common pitfalls to avoid too, from badly planned enquiry to the notion that knowledge organisers can save the world, and offers gentle warnings throughout to help guide us through the maze of purposeful curriculum development.

Paula Owens, teacher, consultant and author

Writing in an engaging and accessible style, Mark manages to pull off the feat of being both theoretically rigorous and eminently practical by sharing case studies from practising teachers and offering signposts to further reading and discussion questions at the end of each chapter.

Essential reading for all teachers of geography, *Powerful Geography* provides a guide to developing and delivering a curriculum with purpose that supports teachers in realising geography's potential to be a truly powerful subject.

Dr Rebecca Kitchen, CPD, Curriculum and Marketing Manager, Geographical Association

This is an original and very welcome book. Mark Enser has fully grasped the nature of powerful knowledge and the three futures approach to thinking about the geography curriculum. These are not analytical concepts that result in recipes for teachers to follow; they are heuristics, developed to enable thought and action.

In producing *Powerful Geography*, Mark manages to convey a sense of geography's significance in the school curriculum – yet he also acknowledges that it is not the last word, and that debates concerning geography education will continue.

David Lambert, Honorary Professor of Geography Education, UCL Institute of Education

Powerful Geography

A Curriculum with Purpose in Practice

Mark Enser

Crown House Publishing Limited
www.crownhouse.co.uk

First published by
Crown House Publishing Limited
Crown Buildings, Bancyfelin, Carmarthen, Wales, SA33 5ND, UK
www.crownhouse.co.uk

and

Crown House Publishing Company LLC
PO Box 2223, Williston, VT 05495, USA
www.crownhousepublishing.com

British Library Cataloguing-in-Publication Data

A catalogue entry for this book is available from the British Library.

Print ISBN 978-178583511-7
Mobi ISBN 978-178583541-4
ePub ISBN 978-178583542-1
ePDF ISBN 978-178583543-8

LCCN 2020951420

Printed and bound in the UK by
Gomer Press, Llandysul, Ceredigion

Acknowledgements

I am incredibly fortunate to teach geography alongside an exceptional team of teachers. Thank you to Rob Messetter for keep my ideas grounded in the reality of having to implement them in the classroom during a busy five-period day, to Sian Parker for the clarity of her suggestions, which are always rooted in experience, and to Karen Amer for her passion for keeping the geography at the heart of all we do.

I am also lucky to work in a school like Heathfield Community College that allows ideas like this to ferment and to be put into practice by teachers on the ground. This does not happen by accident but because of our wonderful leadership team. I would like to thank our head teacher, Caroline Barlow, and my line managers, Becka Lynch and Tom Flower.

Finally, I need to thank my wife Zoe for all her support, patience and understanding, as well as her ideas and suggestions throughout the process of writing this book.

Contents

Introduction

"Anything is geography."

These three words defined the thinking around the geography curriculum when I started teaching in 2004 and, for a while, this seemed hugely exciting. Geography is such a broad discipline that we could – we were told – study anything in our classrooms, put anything into our programmes of study, at least until we had to prepare for an exam specification, and we could call it geography. And so we did. We would create units on the geography of crime in which pupils would consider how different stakeholders felt about a crime that had taken place and, as a result, develop empathy, or study the geography of sport and plot the location of Premier League football stadiums and, as a result, relate the subject to pupils' interests. They could study the geography of fashion and learn about the deplorable conditions of sweatshops and, as a result, hopefully change their shopping habits. What mattered wasn't the content but the *result* of studying it.

The problem is that once we decide that "anything is geography", it starts to become clear that therefore *nothing* is geography. If geography is the development of empathy, the study of things familiar to pupils, and an attempt to make them more conscientious consumers, then what unites it as one subject? How do we define this subject? As I will describe in this book, our subject became lost as it was turned into a vehicle to deliver learning around a range of social issues – according to political priorities – and soft skills to prepare pupils for the needs of an imagined 21st century. Although you could see elements of this in a range of subjects, I think it was a particular issue in geography because it is an unusually messy discipline.

Geography, as a field of study, has a long history stretching back at least as far as the ancient Greeks and the scholar Eratosthenes, who originated the term, coming from the title of his book *Geographica*. However, as an academic university discipline its history only reaches as far back as the 19th century, and much of its expansion occurred in the early 20th century as a way of providing geography teachers to schools. This adolescent subject is still testing its boundaries and seeking to define its role (something which we will discuss further in Chapter 2). As it has gone through this period of reflection it has become too easy for it to be led astray by those who would use it to further their own ends.

These years of confusion are a huge shame as geography has the potential to be a truly *powerful* subject. An understanding of the planet that we call home – how it works, how human and physical processes interact and lead to change – can transform those who study it and open up new vistas from which they can view the world. It is this notion of powerful geography that I wish to explore in this book, building on the idea of powerful knowledge developed by Michael Young and of GeoCapabilities developed by David Lambert and others. I hope that this book will be a practical guide to developing a curriculum with a clear purpose behind it – a purpose which is carried out in practice in the classroom.

I will argue that a powerful curriculum *needs* a clear purpose driving it. Without this clear purpose we will once again get led off into the territory of "anything is geography". The first part of this book will therefore consider the issue of purpose by looking at the role of the school in society and then showing the place that geography occupies within it. We will then consider the history of our subject so as to better understand where we stand today and look in more detail at how we lost sight of geography in the geography classroom. The first part will conclude by discussing how the concepts of powerful knowledge and GeoCapabilities can help us to find our way again.

The second part is a practical guide which illustrates how to put this theory of curriculum purpose into practice. It explores the steps which must be taken to create a powerful geography curriculum by deciding on content and places to be studied, putting the components into a sequence and then using all this to *do* geography. It will also discuss the extent to which we need to consider the future and respond to the concerns of the wider world when planning our curriculum.

It is worth stressing at this point that this book is not just for heads of department and subject leads. The curriculum is not created by one person writing out a programme of study but by each and every teacher in the classroom. The word *curriculum* derives ultimately from a Latin word describing the route of a race, a journey. It is, excitingly for us geography teachers, a map. It is the individual teacher who takes their pupils on this journey and so it is the individual teacher who must take responsibility for understanding their map, especially as they will inevitably alter the route as they teach, finding new tangents to explore and bringing in examples and references from their own lives, interests and experiences. A curriculum is created many times over: set out by national bodies, interpreted by subject associations such as the Geographical Association and Royal Geographical

Society, written by individual school departments, and then created again in the classroom as the teacher brings it to life.

This book is, in part, a response to the worrying trend in education towards the deskilling of teachers. It is becoming an increasingly common expectation for a curriculum to be written by a small team of highly experienced teachers within a school trust and then delivered, as written, by far less experienced teachers across the trust, or even by teachers in schools outside of the trust. We run the risk of creating a culture in which, instead of teachers, we are technicians whose role is simply to deliver the vision of another. Not only will this create problems for the profession, in terms of developing such curriculum-makers of the future and in terms of teacher retention (who went into the profession to be a technician?), but it will also create a weaker curriculum because the teacher who created it needs to be there to bring it to life.

One of the forces that has allowed this deprofessionalisation to occur is the perceived diminishing of the teacher's role in the classroom. Gert Biesta argues that this diminished role came about as a result of the application of constructivist ideas about learning, saying:

> teaching has become increasingly understood as the facilitation of learning rather than as a process where teachers have something to give to their students.[1]

This view of education led to a belief that teachers were simply in the room to draw out of pupils that which they already knew – an idea going back to Socrates. However, Biesta argues that education requires something more than *immanence* (what comes from within): it needs *transcendence* (that which comes from without). Biesta's concern is that we have removed the teacher from education and turned them, at best, into a facilitator of learning or a learning resource. He argues that we need to tell a different story:

> This is a story where teachers are not disposable and dispensable resources for learning, but where they have something to give, where they do not shy away from difficult questions and inconvenient truths, and where they work

1   Gert Biesta, Receiving the gift of teaching: from "learning from" to "being taught by", *Studies in Philosophy and Education* 32(5) (2013): 449–461 at 449.

actively and consistently on the distinction between what is desired and what is desirable, so as to explore what it is that should have authority in our lives.[2]

In this alternative story, schools are not only places of learning, as one can learn anywhere, but are places where pupils are *taught*. It is here that they receive the gift of teaching, the one thing that other social institutions cannot provide.

There is another worrying trend in education, which is the move to make schools agents which serve the needs of wider society. It may be unclear why I deem this worrying, so widespread a belief has this become, but I will argue that the competing and clamouring voices are leading to confusion over the purpose of schools and, as a result, over the purpose of teaching geography. I often find myself thinking back to the phrase coined by the American geographer David Wadley, who calls for academic institutions to be gardens of peace that stand outside the needs of the vibrant neoliberal city.[3] Here, in the garden of peace, we can enjoy the study of the world for its own sake and reach our own conclusions, untroubled by the rest of the world's urgent demands that we serve them. Here in the garden of peace we can be teachers helping to pass on the gift of teaching to our pupils for no reason other than the fact that it is a gift that they have the right to be bequeathed and the fact that it is our duty to bequeath it. What we are left with is a question about what this gift should look like. And that brings us to Part I – the purpose of our curriculum. Enter the garden of peace.

---

2 Biesta, Receiving the gift of teaching, 459.
3 David A. Wadley, The garden of peace, *Annals of the Association of American Geographers* 98(3) (2008): 650–685.

Part I
Purpose

Chapter 1

School – what is it good for?

Different possible purposes

One of the problems we have in shaping a curriculum in our schools is that there is scant agreement over what schools should be trying to achieve. This leads to various voices all trying to have their say and insisting that schools should fulfil a function that they deem vital. For example:

- Schools attempt to provide childcare for parents so that they can work (look at the chaos that results if schools are closed).

- They are asked to raise children and equip them with life skills (see the endless calls for children to be taught how to cook basic meals or to learn to garden).

- There is an expectation that they will develop pupils' character (to make them resilient, or equip them with grit or a growth mindset).

- They need to cultivate pupils' moral character (so that they have empathy and behave in a socially responsible way).

- We expect them to equip young people with skills that make them employable (these "employability skills" vary but include a mix of practical capabilities and favourable personality traits, such as the ability to work well in teams or be creative).

- They need to look after children's mental health and make them happy (or teach them how to be happy and "mindful").

- And, in amongst all of this, they need to provide a broad and balanced academic curriculum that equips them with qualifications that demonstrate their ability in a range of subjects.

Even if we were to strip all these expectations away and argue that the primary purpose of a school is, as discussed in the introduction, to be a place where pupils are taught, we are still left with the question about what they should be taught. As Gert Biesta says:

> Perhaps the briefest way to put it is to say that the point of education is not that students learn [...] In contrast I wish to suggest that the point of education is that students learn something, that they learn it for a reason, and that they learn it from someone.[1]

He goes on to argue that schools fulfil three functions within society:

1 **Qualification** – in which pupils learn to *do* something through the acquisition of knowledge and skills.

2 **Socialisation** – which here refers to the initiation into different traditions or *ways* of doing and being.

3 **Subjectification** – in which pupils become the subjects of initiatives and actions rather than the object of the initiatives and actions of others.

In other words, schools are places in which pupils are taught the knowledge and skills that allow them to do what they could not do before. They are taught how to think in new ways, apply knowledge in different ways (mathematically, geographically, historically, etc.) and develop the capabilities to use this knowledge as they see fit in the future.

This purpose of schooling seems fairly straightforward and uncontentious but, as this chapter will show, nothing could be further from the truth. The purpose and methods of schooling have been debated for centuries and have left a legacy of confusion and a tangle of competing ideologies that need to be cleared away if we are ever to create our garden of peace – with a clear purpose at its heart – in our schools.

1 Gert Biesta, What is education for? On good education, teacher judgement, and educational professionalism, *European Journal of Education* 50(1) (2015): 75–87 at p. 76.

Uncertain foundations

Education – specifically the purpose thereof – was on shaky ground from the very start due to the influence of one of the founders of Western philosophy. Education, according to Socrates, should be concerned with teaching the young to be moral creatures who can differentiate between truth and lies, good and evil, right and wrong, etc. Education was about the *examined life* – people must be aware of the reasons why they make the decisions they make. This was, in part, because education was seen as something that was only necessary for the ruling classes, and Socrates, along with Plato, was concerned with how to create just societies by ensuring these ruling classes made just decisions.

Perhaps one of Socrates' biggest influences on education today is the idea that the role of the teacher isn't really to teach at all, but is to draw out of the pupil that which is already inside of them through questioning that would lead to some sort of revelation. This is the immanence, also termed a *maieutic* process, discussed in the introduction. it is an idea of education that may make sense if you are largely concerned with the ethics of human actions, starting by exploring the fundamental principle of fairness and then questioning to help the pupil realise how this might apply to complex moral problems, but as a principle it is hard to apply if you want to teach your pupil something outside their own field of experience, and this would include most of what we think of as geography.

It would be very difficult to use a maieutic process to teach something like the movement of the earth's tectonic plates. Our understanding of how plates move is based on the careful study of the lithosphere by many generations of scientists, geologists and geographers. This knowledge isn't within our pupils waiting to be teased out; it needs to be imparted in one way or another, and this idea of imparting knowledge is antithetical to the Romantic ideals that remain at the heart of our educational values.

The Romantic ideals

One of the most influential voices of the modern era is that of Jean-Jacques Rousseau. His thinking and writing influenced the French and American revolutions, the poetry of the Romantics and some of the underlying ideas and values that have survived in the education world into the 21st century. His views can perhaps be seen most directly in the work of the founders of progressive and constructivist schools of thought in education: Jean Piaget, John Dewey and the often-overlooked Herbert Spencer.[2]

It is in *Émile* – part novel, part teaching handbook – that Rousseau most clearly sets out his vision for education.[3] The book, over some 500 pages, describes the education the protagonist receives at the hands of his tutor (a barely disguised stand-in for the author himself, who, it should be remembered, had abandoned five of his own children at foundling hospitals shortly after their births), who raises him and guides him from birth to the age of 25. Central to his approach is the belief that education should happen as close to nature as possible, away from the corruptions of wider society. This natural education would be led by the needs and desires of the pupil. They would learn by following their own lines of enquiry and pursuing their own interests so that they can discover things for themselves. They would not be told the answers by a teacher, nor have knowledge imparted to them, but the teacher would act as the guide by their side, setting up situations in which the pupil could learn for themselves based on what they already know.

Despite the Romantic ideals of freedom and pupil-led learning, a clear curriculum is still presented by Rousseau. Émile's freedoms are largely illusionary, with his tutor having a very clear plan regarding what he should eventually learn and what his character should become. Everything that Émile purportedly "discovers" for himself is the result of having been closely led to that conclusion by his tutor. There is also little in *Émile* that suggests how this vision of education might be rolled out to the masses. Everything in the book is predicated on the idea that a tutor can craft a highly personalised curriculum to meet the needs of a single pupil, leading them to the next stage of learning at the exact point at which they are ready for it. It is hard to envisage how this could happen for a teacher in front

2 Kieran Egan, *Getting It Wrong from the Beginning: Our Progressivist Inheritance from Herbert Spencer, John Dewey, and Jean Piaget* (New Haven, CT: Yale University Press, 2002).
3 Jean-Jacques Rousseau, *Émile, Or On Education*, tr. Barbara Foxley (London: Dent, 1911 [1762]).

of a class of 30 pupils, especially in a secondary school where they might see hundreds of pupils over the course of a week. This approach lacks the pragmatism needed for mass education.

Pragmatism

In Rousseauian and ancient Greek thinking, education is designed for a very different audience. Socrates and Plato were largely concerned with educating their society's future rulers, and even by the Romantic era most writing on education focused on its provision only for a small ruling class. For the majority of people, a school-based education was not deemed necessary. Most children learnt what their parents knew or were apprenticed to a trade within their community.

This had started to change by the end of the 19th century. As every geographer can tell you, employment structures were changing, and people were flowing out of the countryside and into the cities. It was no longer enough for young people to rely on received knowledge from their parents; society needed them to be prepared to go into a much wider range of occupations that often demanded at least basic levels of literacy and numeracy. School could no longer be the preserve of the elite; there needed to be schooling for the masses.

This posed some problems for those putting together a curriculum for these new schools. A classical curriculum, which provided the kind of education enjoyed by those creating policies and practices for new schools, had been designed for the leisured classes. This curriculum focused on classical history and natural sciences, perfect for a gentleman who wanted to appear cultured at parties, but – it was felt – lacking the utility for the working classes (or for women, who didn't require this form of education to fulfil the role society had allotted them). This desire for utility in education was nothing new. Philosopher John Locke, writing in the late 17th century, favoured a utilitarian education, although his definition of utilitarianism made room for Latin, natural philosophy and classical history. Much of this was to be swept away by the pragmatists at the start of the 20th century.[4]

This desire for pragmatism seems to have stemmed from two beliefs. Firstly, that schools should be providing an education that meets the needs of society, largely

4 Nicholas Tate, *What Is Education For? The View of the Great Thinkers and Their Relevance Today* (Woodbridge: John Catt Educational, 2015).

by training children ready for employment and possibly developing their character in such a way as to be useful to wider society. This was a view shared by the hugely influential educationalist John Dewey, who argued that decisions on curriculum should be based on the criterion of social worth.[5] The curriculum would therefore focus on functional literacy and numeracy – rather than on literature and mathematics – and on practical skills involving technology and practical applications of science, rather than on the arts and humanities.

The second argument for pragmatism was made in the 1926 Hadow Report (printed in 1927) that looked into English education. The report stated that the classical, liberal education of the past was simply unsuitable for the kinds of children now attending school, claiming:

> Many more, without having any clear idea what they will do when they leave school, feel ill at ease in an atmosphere of books and lessons, and are eager to turn to some form of practical and constructive work, in which they will not merely be learners, but doers, and, in a small way, creators.[6]

According to this view, it was concern for children from working-class backgrounds that was driving changes in the curriculum: concern that they were being given the education of a different culture – the knowledge *of* the powerful – that would mean very little to them and so excite no particular interest in what they were learning. We see here a harking back to the ideas of the Romantics: that the curriculum should be based around pupils' interests and guided by their own experiences and desires.

What these two arguments meant in practice was that both the traditional "right" of society and the progressive "left" were pulling education in the same direction: away from the view that being educated was an intrinsic good and that everyone should have access to the same deep well of knowledge from which to drink, and towards utilitarianism and the idea that a different education should be offered to pupils depending on their own individual needs and backgrounds. This view was to have far-reaching consequences for both children and wider society.

5   Latasha Holt, John Dewey: a look at his contributions to curriculum, *Academicus International Scientific Journal* 21 (2020): 142–150.
6   Board of Education, *Report of the Consultative Committee on the Education of the Adolescent* [The 1926 Hadow Report] (London: His Majesty's Stationery Office, 1927), p. 84. Available at: http://www.educationengland.org.uk/documents/hadow1926/hadow1926.html.

Does it matter?

It would be easy to argue that the thoughts of the ancient Greeks and an 18th-century French philosopher are of little concern to those of us writing geography curricula today. However, their words and ideas continue to resonate in the often-unexamined assumptions that many people hold about education. Kieran Egan makes a convincing case about how our attitudes, especially in the UK and North America, can be traced back to the late-19th-century work of Herbert Spencer.[7] Egan argues that Spencer continued the work of Rousseau but imbued those ideas with scientific authority. Like Rousseau, he wanted to see natural methods of learning that reflected how children learnt through play and developed language. As Egan explains:

> Once methods and curricula more hospitable to children's natural modes of learning were in place, their desire for knowledge would be released and a revolution in learning would occur.[8]

He goes on to point out that our various education systems have dedicated huge amounts of time, energy and ingenuity to trying to make education better resemble a Rousseau-inspired classroom of spontaneous learning, but without the promised revolution ever occurring.

In the geography classroom we can see this influence in attempts to have pupils find as much knowledge as they can through discovery via enquiry methodology and the avoidance of simply telling them what they need to know. We can see the influence in the calls for us to have pupils outside and learning in the field as much as possible or to base our curriculum on pupils' interests – for example, by including units on the geography of sport or the geography of fashion. We even hear calls that we should survey our pupils to discover their precise interests so that we can tailor the curriculum to them. These ideas stem from that desire to do as educationalist William Heard Kilpatrick demanded: make schools places of experience.[9]

7   Egan, *Getting it Wrong from the Beginning.*
8   Egan, *Getting it Wrong from the Beginning,* p. 38.
9   William Heard Kilpatrick, *Education for a Changing Civilization: Three Lectures Delivered on the Luther Kellogg Foundation at Rutgers University, 1926* (New York: Arno Press and the New York Times, 1971).

The fundamental flaw here is that by basing our curriculum on the experiences that pupils can readily access, or have already had, we don't add anything new; they are denied access to knowledge from beyond their own narrow range of experiences. To return to Egan again, he points out:

> Knowledge exists only as a function of living tissue … it affects how we think and feel and education is about precisely improving these things.[10]

Whether we are aware of it or not, the practice of attempting to base the curriculum on pupils' existing experience originates in the ideas of Socrates. Biesta argues that we need to move away from seeing teaching as maieutic and instead realise its *transcendent* nature: that teachers bring something new to their pupils through a process of *revelation*.[11] Our fears of accepting a mantle of authority in the classroom, and of accepting our role as subject experts who are passing on the gift of knowledge to the next generation, leaves us *having* to base the curriculum on what our pupils bring to the classroom. If they don't have the knowledge already within them, we cannot draw it out; we would be forced to impart something, and therefore accept a very different power dynamic than years of subtle conditioning has allowed us to see as acceptable.

Although this concern over power is completely understandable, the impact of this stance on knowledge and curriculum has had the most detrimental effect on those in society with the least power. American educationalist E. D. Hirsch, Jr uses the example of France to show what happens when the education system changes to avoid perceived issues with transmission of the wrong type of knowledge.[12]

As Hirsch explains, until the late 1980s France had one of the highest performing and most equitable education systems in the world. Regardless of a pupil's background, they could expect a good chance to do well at school. All schools were expected to teach the same common curriculum and there was a great deal of similarity in how this curriculum was delivered. However, the influence of the same kind of Romanticism, combined with the same kind of pragmatism, that affected the English education system was taking hold in France. There were worries that the system was equitable *enough* and it was hypothesised that this was because

---

10 Egan, *Getting it Wrong from the Beginning*, p. 68.
11 Biesta, Receiving the gift of teaching.
12 E. D. Hirsch, Jr, *Why Knowledge Matters: Rescuing Our Children from Failed Educational Theories* (Cambridge, MA: Harvard University Press, 2016).

the common curriculum taught the culture of the powerful and so benefitted them more. It was decided that the common curriculum should be abolished and, instead, control given to each local district, who could then decide on what their pupils should learn and how. The curriculum could thus better reflect the interests and background of the pupils and should therefore lead to better education for all.

It didn't. Instead what happened was that *all* pupils did worse, at least according to the baseline tests introduced by the French ministry of education that compared pupil outcomes in 1987, 1997 and 2007. However, the more economically advantaged pupils did less badly in 2007 than their disadvantaged peers, and as a result the gap became wider. The more advantaged pupils were protected from the full effects of the changes. Their parents could still give them access to the culturally rich education that was now being denied to less advantaged children. The desire to correct a power imbalance had backfired.

A confused curriculum

What we are left with is a series of values, beliefs and ideologies that lie unspoken and unexamined behind the decisions that shape our curriculum. We assume that:

- We should draw knowledge out of our pupils.

- Education should be directed by the interests of our pupils.

- Our curriculum should reflect the needs of society.

If we were to follow these precepts, we would have to base topics on our pupils' own prior experiences so that we could be sure we were drawing out, rather than imparting, knowledge. We would avoid more complex ideas that were too abstract and far-removed from their own lives. It would be easier to focus on issues that they would have a strong reaction to – deforestation, migration, climate change, etc. – but the content would focus on their own feelings about the topic, rather than any exploration of the geographical complexity surrounding it, as this complexity couldn't be drawn out of their existing knowledge.

We would also have to try to personalise our curriculum to reflect local, or even individual, interests. We would include topics that we think will appeal to the demographic in our classrooms – the geography of sport, the geography of fashion, the geography of crime, for example ... perhaps we would try to give pupils different options about what they studied and how, so as to best replicate Spencer's natural modes of learning.

Then we would have to ensure that what we taught focused not on the subject itself – as that is unlikely to have much immediate utility to employers – and instead concentrate on creating a curriculum that emphasises the "soft" or "generic" skills – such as group work or creativity – that the economy demands. Or we might decide that we need to cover those issues that society currently deems to be worthwhile – climate change, plastic use and knife crime might all find their way on to the curriculum, but with a focus not on the underpinning geography but on simply trying to shape our pupils' behaviour.

I would suggest that to some extent this is what has happened to the geography curriculum in schools up and down not only England, but in the curricula of schools around the world. Too often we have lost sight of the intrinsic value in studying our subject and been led astray by the calls for it to serve some extrinsic function. It has been warped as we have bent and twisted to try to teach a subject so rich in the knowledge of previous generations without doing anything so basic as to dare to impart this knowledge from teacher to pupil. We have been fooled into believing that our subject might interest *us*, but that *they* need to have it hidden from them behind a screen of relevance, as though the next generation cannot possibly be interested in the wider world for its own sake.

Case study: Sarah Larsen

It was September 2012. I had just returned to teaching after a three-year career break to care for my two small children. However, in that relatively short space of time, something had changed. When I left the classroom, I had done so thinking how much I would miss standing at the front, being paid to talk about the subject I was so passionate about, and watch as I was able to transfer some of the awe and wonder that geography had to offer to the pupils.

Yet upon my return to the profession I discovered that my role had changed. No longer did I need to be the "sage on the stage", but more the "guide from the side". The fashion now seemed to be to let pupils discover and construct new knowledge for themselves, through activities such as scavenger hunts, card sorts (bonus points if you got the pupils to cut the cards out themselves first as this also kept them busy!), games which were tenuously linked to something geographical, carousel activities, information packs, tablet lessons … I could go on. I was to spend as little time as possible talking to the class, and indeed I was timed during lesson observations in order to ensure that the pupils were working independently for as long as possible, trying to make sense of often tricky-to-grasp new material. These activities, I was told, would form the constituent parts of a lesson which Ofsted would grade "outstanding". The pupils would be engaged, there would be a buzz in the room, they would be busy *doing* something …

The difficulty was – and this is something that we as a profession now acknowledge thanks to a shift in thinking centred around evidence from cognitive science – that none of these activities, or indeed the reasons given for doing them, involved very much *learning*. And that is ultimately what we as teachers are in the business of doing. This style of teaching has come to be known by several names over the last few decades: discovery learning, constructivism, enquiry-based learning – all of which put the pupil at the centre of solving problems and making sense of new material. And therein lies the problem. Our pupils are novice learners. Many will lack any prior knowledge or the ability to bring to mind the knowledge that they *do* have in order to connect it to the new material, and thus they are unable to build on their mental schema sufficiently in order to make sense of the learning and make it stick in their long-term memories. Without the teacher's expert guidance, misconceptions will arise which will need to be unpicked later – and the load placed on pupils' working memories will be too great. They will be too preoccupied with trying to get to grips with the difficulty of the problem for any meaningful learning to take place. Both Barak Rosenshine[13] and Paul Kirschner et al.[14] discuss how the most effective teachers instruct pupils, chunk new material, and guide, model and question so that cognitive overload does not take place. Pupils are then made

---

13 Barak Rosenshine, Principles of instruction: research-based strategies that all teachers should know, *American Educator* 36(1) (2012): 12–19, 39. Available at: https://www.aft. org/sites/default/files/periodicals/Rosenshine.pdf.
14 Paul A. Kirschner, John Sweller and Richard E. Clark, Why minimal guidance during instruction does not work: an analysis of the failure of constructivist, discovery, project-based, experiential, and inquiry-based teaching, *Educational Psychologist* 41(2) (2006): 75–86.

to think hard by engaging in deliberate practice and applying the new content to a task or practising their new skill so as to lead to mastery.

As a consequence of becoming interested in research-informed practice in the last couple of years, and engaging in conversations on Twitter and at educational events about how this might look in the classroom, the laborious job of making resources for the pupils to use independently in order to make sense of new material – which often led to off-task chatter, misbehaviour and misunderstandings, which left me exasperated, exhausted and ultimately resulted in very little learning – is now a thing of the past. Despite having been teaching for 23 years, it is only relatively recently that I, along with a growing number of teachers, have engaged with the world of educational research, some of which has been around for decades. This evidence-informed approach to the profession is gradually allowing us to cut out the fads and the nonsense that many of us never felt truly comfortable with in the first place. Our assertions about what works have been given much more weight and we have been allowed to get back to common-sense basics and engaging our pupils through the beauty and simplicity of our subject. The belief that pupils could not possibly find the subject matter itself engaging without the need to disguise it in an all-singing, all-dancing activity in which the teacher is superfluous to requirements seems to finally be being put to bed. Teachers are, once more, free to do what they are experts at – teaching!

Sarah Larsen is a geography teacher, blogger and speaker living in Sussex. She tweets as @sarahlarsen74.

As teachers, we tend to be too busy dealing with the day-to-day demands of the job to be able to step back and look at the underlying history that shapes what we do. Much of what I have discussed in this chapter just rolls on beneath our notice. Only by exposing it to the light can we hope to examine our own assumptions about the purpose of schooling, and therefore of our subject, and then move forward. By the end of Part I, I hope that we will have achieved just that. But, for now, let us have a look inside the geography classroom and consider the role that knowledge plays there.

Questions

- Review the curriculum you currently teach. To what extent does it try to include things that are seen as being more relevant to your pupils in some way? To what extent is this useful?

- How is your teaching influenced by the Socratic idea of drawing information out of pupils?

- Can you see the influences of Rousseau's ideas in your practice or in the practice of others?

Further reading

Alex Standish and Alka Sehgal Cuthbert (eds), *What Should Schools Teach? Disciplines, Subjects and the Pursuit of Truth* (London: UCL Institute of Education Press, 2017).

Nicholas Tate, *What Is Education For? The View of the Great Thinkers and Their Relevance Today* (Woodbridge: John Catt Educational, 2015).

Chapter 2

Approaches to knowledge

Why knowledge sits at the heart of education

As we saw in Chapter 1, there is little agreement about the purpose that schools should serve. There are those who see us as doing little more than preparing the next generation of employees by equipping them with skills for the workplace; whereas others want us to develop our pupils' characters so that they hold certain values or develop attributes which are deemed desirable (by the powers that be, of course, not by the pupils themselves). Some of us might argue that the purpose of schools is to pass on the accumulated wisdom of previous generations to the next. However, whatever view you put forward about the purpose of schooling, there is one thing they all have in common – *knowledge*.

Ultimately, schools exist to make pupils more knowledgeable than they would have otherwise been. This knowledge might be relevant to future employment (how to write a formal letter, operate a lathe or work as part of a team, perhaps) or it might shape how pupils will behave and the values they will hold throughout their lives (knowledge of the dangers of single-use plastics or of the flaws in racist ideology, for example). It could even be what Gert Biesta calls *subjectification*: the knowledge of ourselves and our agency to affect the world.[1] It could, of course, also be knowledge in the way in which we more commonly use the word in a geographical context: the knowledge of the world and how it operates (knowledge of how an oxbow lake formed or the knowledge of push and pull factors that drive migration, for example).

Because knowledge plays such a central role in what we do in schools, we need to have a good understanding of different types of knowledge if we are going to create a curriculum with purpose. We need to know which kinds of knowledge we

1 Biesta, What is education for?

are trying to develop in our pupils, and to what end, as this will shape the curricular decisions we make. This chapter will consider these different types of knowledge in the context of the geography curriculum, the debates that exist over the types of knowledge that should be taught, and what this means for us as we look to develop a purposeful curriculum.

Defining knowledge

The educationalist Jerome Bruner developed nine tenets that explain how schools can meet the learning needs of their pupils.[2] One of these, the "instrumentalism" tenet, states that children need to be supported in constructing a model of the world which will enable them to make sense of their experience of living in it. He suggests that what pupils learn through the curriculum and the methods chosen to teach it – the pedagogy – will be determined by the type of knowledge that is seen as important. One common way of classifying knowledge is as either *propositional* or *procedural*.

Propositional knowledge is often thought of as facts, and the geography curriculum tends to be full of them. The stages of the demographic transition model would be propositional knowledge, as would the responses to Typhoon Haiyan. This type of knowledge is sometimes known as "declarative" knowledge: things that you can declare to be true (whether they are actually true or not is beside the point). Although propositional knowledge is sometimes demonised as the dry accumulation of isolated pieces of information, it is the basis of understanding. If we want pupils to understand why some countries struggle to respond to disasters, knowing how the Philippines responded to Typhoon Haiyan is useful. If we want pupils to understand – and be able to express their understanding of – the links between economic development and population change, it will help if they have knowledge of the model that shows the connection.

Procedural knowledge is sometimes confused with *skills* but, strictly speaking, it is the knowledge of how to do things, which – with practice – *become* skills. For example, you might have the procedural knowledge of how to drive a car and will

---

2 Jerome Bruner, Tenets to understand a cultural perspective on learning. In Bob Moon, Ann Shelton Mayes and Steven Hutchinson (eds), *Teaching, Learning and Curriculum in Secondary Schools: A Reader* (Abingdon and New York: RoutledgeFalmer, 2002), pp. 10–24.

become more skilled at doing so through practice. In geography, procedural knowledge would include how to draw and interpret climate graphs, carry out fieldwork, how to design an effective questionnaire, or write up the findings of an enquiry. The definition of procedural knowledge could also be extended to include more abstract concepts such as how to be creative or work well as a team.

One type of procedural knowledge that might warrant its own distinct subcategory is metacognition. This is the knowledge of what you know and how you came to know it. It is sometimes referred to as your ability to "think about thinking". It would include knowing about effective study skills and what to do if you get stuck on a problem, including the strategies you have at your disposal to work around it. This can be widened further to other forms of self-regulation, which include knowing what motivates you and the types of behaviour that will lead to better learning.

Jenny Leach and Bob Moon suggest that as well as these three types of knowledge (propositional, procedural and metacognitive) we should also add the categories of *informal* and *impressionistic* knowledge.[3] Informal knowledge is sometimes called *tacit* knowledge. It may form from experience in a way that makes it very difficult to put into words. For example, a person might have developed the tacit knowledge that there is a difficult balance to reach between economic growth and environmental concerns but not have the formal, propositional knowledge to support this idea or articulate it in more detail. It will be based on nuances that they have picked up from various sources over the years, without their explicit awareness. Impressionistic knowledge is quite similar in that it can be difficult to articulate. It refers to the impression that specific experiences may cast upon us – that may therefore shape us – but in ways that do not necessarily lead to formal knowledge. We might feel something, but we cannot declare that we know it. For example, seeing an emotional appeal for emergency aid in a famine-stricken part of North Africa might leave a lasting impression on you about the nature of that place, but with little other context it might be very difficult to say exactly what you now know about it. Leach and Moon argue that:

> It is this type of knowledge with its hesitations and uncertainties that can cause much misgiving, perhaps to the point of being shut out in formal learning and teaching situations.[4]

3 Jenny Leach and Bob Moon, *The Power of Pedagogy* (London: Sage, 2008).
4 Moon and Leach, *The Power of Pedagogy*, p. 95.

This tacit and impressionistic knowledge is sometimes referred to as *everyday* knowledge to distinguish it from the formal knowledge that is dealt with by schools. Geography educationalists Simon Catling and Fran Martin argue that this everyday knowledge – or, as they term it, ethno-geographies of children – is often not given its rightful place in the geography curriculum.[5] They contend that this is particularly the case in primary schools, where a lack of subject-specialism may leave the teacher ill-equipped to teach geography as an academic discipline and lead to them trying to deliver it as a body of *information*, rather than *understanding*, about the world. They suggest that by focusing on the everyday knowledge that both pupils and teachers bring to the classroom, non-specialists will be better equipped to focus on developing the pupils' understanding of geography as a discipline. Everyday knowledge may also be used as a way into more abstract and conceptual ideas within the subject. For example, a pupil's own experiences of swimming in the sea and noticing how they often get out further down the beach than the point at which they entered might be used to introduce the idea of long-shore drift.

Three futures and powerful knowledge

The everyday knowledge that a pupil picks up from their own experiences is often contrasted with powerful knowledge. The term "powerful knowledge" was coined by sociologist Michael Young to distinguish the knowledge that he felt schools should be teaching from the knowledge of the powerful. During the 1970s Young had been very influential in sharing his view that the knowledge taught in schools belonged to the powerful in society, and so benefitted them the most. Those without power did not see themselves reflected in the taught curriculum and so were less likely to succeed in school. Teaching the knowledge of the powerful therefore widened the gap further.

However, by the new millennium Young's views had shifted dramatically. He saw that attempts to avoid teaching the knowledge of the powerful to the children of the least powerful did not lead to the gap closing; it continued to widen. All that was happening was that these children were missing out not only on the

5   Simon Catling and Fran Martin, Contesting powerful knowledge: the primary geography curriculum as an articulation between academic and children's (ethno-) geographies, *The Curriculum Journal* 22(3) (2011): 317–335.

knowledge of the powerful but on powerful knowledge as well. As Hirsch noted in his case study of the overhaul of the French education system (see Chapter 1), the children of the powerful continue to access powerful knowledge regardless of what happens to state education. Young's about-turn signalled a move away from a social-constructivist to a social-realist view of knowledge, mirroring a shift of opinion in the education world more widely.[6]

A social-constructivist view of knowledge holds that what we know is always created by the individual and unique to them: there is, therefore, no such thing as an objective truth that can be passed from one person to another. This view was a reaction to the previously prevailing dogma – that of positivism – which stated that the world could be subjected to observation and testing, and that absolute truths could be reached and transmitted. Young termed these two competing views Future 1 and Future 2:[7]

- **Future 1** – Knowledge is fixed and absolute (positivist). The role of the school is to transmit this given knowledge from those who have the knowledge to those who do not. Education is seen as worthwhile for its own sake and concentrates on making individuals more knowledgeable.

- **Future 2** – Knowledge is created by each individual (constructivist). The role of the school is to facilitate the pupil in creating their own understanding of the world, preferably by pursuing their own personalised curriculum that reflects their interests. Education is instrumental, a means to an (often vocational) end and concentrates on developing competencies and skills.

In terms of types of knowledge, Future 1 concentrates on formal procedural and propositional knowledge whilst Future 2 emphasises informal tacit and impressionistic knowledge. What Young did was suggest a move away from the positivist–constructivist dichotomy towards a social-realist perspective.

Social realism accepts that knowledge is constructed and contested but denies that this means we cannot select knowledge to pass from one generation to the next. Instead, it suggests that knowledge about the world is constructed within the traditions and perspectives of subject disciplines. There are clear rules about how that knowledge can be contested and improved. What we can identify is the best

6   Michael Young, *Bringing Knowledge Back in: From Social Constructivism to Social Realism in the Sociology of Education* (Abingdon and New York: Routledge, 2008).
7   Michael Young and David Lambert, *Knowledge and the Future School: Curriculum and Social Justice* (London: Bloomsbury, 2014).

knowledge available to us at the moment from within those disciplines. The knowledge produced by subject disciplines is specialist knowledge and stands in contrast to the everyday knowledge that we might pick up in our day-to-day lives. It is from this body of specialist knowledge that Young says schools should be building their curriculum. This is not, he explains, because this knowledge has a greater *value* but because it is knowledge that will otherwise be denied to pupils. Everyday knowledge is not otherwise denied to them.[8]

Michael Young and Johan Muller list four features of specialist knowledge.[9]

1   Specialist knowledge is systematically revisable. It is always being challenged and updated from within the discipline as part of a quest for truth.

2   Specialist knowledge is emergent. It is produced by social conditions and contexts but can't simply be reduced to those conditions and contexts. It transcends them.

3   Specialist knowledge is real. It says something in a reliable and robust way and isn't purely subjective and relative.

4   Specialist knowledge is material and social. It is taken from disciplines which produce knowledge within their own epistemic foundations.

One way of defining powerful knowledge, then, is through the way in which it is created. It is powerful because it is more likely to be reliable than knowledge formed from one person's experience is. Geographer David Lambert explains it like this:

> In short it is knowledge that is created by specialist communities or disciplines: all knowledge is a human construction, but powerful knowledge is made in accordance with some rigorous and demanding procedures and practices, put in place to test knowledge claims potentially to destruction. These state of art epistemic practices are established to ensure that knowledge created is reliable and truthful: indeed, that it is the best it can be.[10]

8   Young and Lambert, *Knowledge and the Future School*, pp. 74–75.
9   Michael Young and Johan Muller, Three educational scenarios for the future: lessons for the sociology of knowledge, *European Journal of Education* 45(1) (2010): 11–27.
10 David Lambert, Curriculum thinking, "capabilities" and the place of geographical knowledge in schools, *Journal of Educational Research on Social Studies* 81 (2014): 1–11 at 7.

Every academic subject is on its own quest for truth as it takes what is already known and challenges and contests it to produce new knowledge that in time will also be challenged, contested and changed. This process produces *disciplinary knowledge*, much of which would be inaccessible to anyone outside of that discipline without it being taught by someone with access to both it *and* pedagogical knowledge. The ability to combine subject and pedagogical knowledge is at the heart of the role of the teacher.

It is also possible to understand powerful knowledge through what it allows people to do: the capabilities it produces in them. Specialist knowledge is powerful because it takes pupils beyond their everyday experiences and allows them to not only understand the world but also to understand how their understanding came about and how it might be challenged and changed. Young argues that it allows young people to engage in politics and wider debates about the world, saying:

> **Powerful knowledge refers to what the knowledge can do or what intellectual power it gives to those who have access to it. Powerful knowledge provides more reliable explanations and new ways of thinking about the world and acquiring it and can provide learners with a language for engaging in political, moral, and other kinds of debates.[11]**

He also argues that powerful knowledge is needed if people are to challenge authority[12] and to predict, explain and envisage alternatives.[13]

Alaric Maude examines the various capabilities created by powerful knowledge, as discussed by Young, and suggests that geographical knowledge is powerful if it enables people to:[14]

1   Discover new ways of thinking.

2   Better explain and understand the natural and social worlds.

3   Think about alternative futures and what they could do to influence them.

4   Have some power over their own knowledge.

....

11 Young, *Bringing Knowledge Back in*, p. 14.
12 Young, *Bringing Knowledge Back in*, p. 14.
13 Young and Lambert, *Knowledge and the Future School*.
14 Alaric Maude, What might powerful geographical knowledge look like?, *Geography* 101(2) (2016): 70–76 at 72.

5   Be able to engage in current debates of significance.

6   Go beyond the limits of their personal experience.

We will consider how this applies to the geography curriculum in Part II.

Debates on building knowledge

The role that knowledge plays, or could play, in education is highly contested as seen through the Future 1–Future 2 dichotomy. One "side" argues that knowledge is fixed and absolute whilst the other argues that it is relative and constructed only by the individual. Whilst such debates may often be confined to the papers produced by sociologists, philosophers and educationalists, they do sometimes spill out into how we as teachers approach the curriculum. This often manifests in three contested areas, exemplified by the questions:

1   What is the role of "everyday knowledge"?

2   Whose knowledge?

3   Should we follow a skills curriculum?

As already discussed, *powerful* knowledge is often defined in contrast to *everyday* knowledge. The former is based on the knowledge created in subject disciplines in a formal and regulated manner, whereas the latter emerges from individual experience. There are two ways in which everyday knowledge may be approached in the curriculum. The first, and most common, is as a starting point to then venture away from into something further from personal experience – moving from the concrete to the abstract, as educational psychologist Jerome Bruner suggests.[15] Pupils may struggle to understand the way in which glaciers shape the land through plucking and freeze-thaw action but they may have experienced getting their tongue stuck to ice or seen that the water in a plastic bottle expands when put in the freezer overnight. In this way, everyday experience becomes a source of analogies.

A more controversial debate over everyday knowledge centres on the role it should play in dictating the content of the curriculum itself. Should topics be

---

15 Jerome S. Bruner, *Toward a Theory of Instruction* (Cambridge, MA: Belknap Press, 1966).

chosen that reflect the interests and experiences of the pupils? Whose knowledge should we teach? Theirs or our own? The aim, according to the social-realist approach, is that we teach neither their knowledge (which they already have) or our own personal knowledge. We are teaching the knowledge created in academic disciplines which are engaged in their own quests for truth.

This is not to downplay the importance of the everyday knowledge that pupils bring to the classroom, it is just that it doesn't need to be given to them; they are bringing it to us. Everyday knowledge can make an excellent starting point in the geography curriculum as it allows us to contrast what they already know, or believe, about the world with perspectives from elsewhere. For example, their own knowledge of water resource issues in the UK (occasional hosepipe bans and warnings about overconsumption) could be a useful starting point when looking at the very different issues facing countries suffering from economic scarcity.

One debate that we should be aware of when planning our powerful geography curriculum is often framed as knowledge vs skills. There is a concern that by focusing on making pupils more knowledgeable we may be making them less skilled. This debate can be seen played out between the Future 1 and the Future 2 views of curriculum: Future 1 wants little more than the transmission of a body of knowledge, and Future 2 wants little more than the development of generic competencies and/or skills. Future 3 comes some way towards resolving this debate.

If we consider that a skill is something that develops with practice, we can see that it is not something we can teach. What we can teach is the procedural knowledge that then allows the pupils to practice the skill. For example, the skill of describing distribution on a choropleth map is based on procedural knowledge of:

- How choropleth maps work.

- Location.

- How geographers describe distribution.

The ability to do this well – the skill – will come when they have the opportunity to practise applying this procedural knowledge over and over again until it becomes second nature. What is needed is an approach that teaches the propositional knowledge and then ensures that there is time for pupils to practise with and return to it time and time again.

What is "geographical knowledge"?

We can conclude, then, that the purpose of schools is to teach the knowledge that pupils would not otherwise have access to. This is powerful, academic knowledge that needs recontextualising and teaching by an expert through a carefully constructed curriculum. Each academic discipline is on its own quest for truth and looks at the world in a very different way, and this is reflected in the way in which we organise the timetable into different subjects. In our subject, we aim to teach geographical knowledge.

This is the knowledge that should transform how our pupils see the world. It should enable them to understand how the world was shaped and how it continues to be shaped by both human and physical processes, and how these processes shape us in return. Bringing this together should mean that they gain an understanding of places and the features that make them unique, but also those things they have in common. Pupils should develop the disciplinary knowledge to be able to interrogate geographical claims, or claims about geographical issues, and not take assertions on face value.

Whilst this may seem uncontentious, the battle over the nature of school geography has a long history and it is still being waged, which brings us to our next chapter on the changing nature of school geography.

Questions

- To what extent do you feel you achieve a balance between different forms of knowledge in your curriculum?

- Do you agree that powerful knowledge is distinct from everyday knowledge? Why (or why not)?

- Reviewing the curriculum you teach, how do you think it fits into the three futures model outlined by Young and Muller?

Further reading

Michael Young and David Lambert, *Knowledge and the Future School: Curriculum and Social Justice* (London: Bloomsbury, 2014).

Graham Butt and Gemma Collins, Understanding the gap between schools and universities. In Mark Jones and David Lambert (eds), *Debates in Geography Education*, 2nd edn (Abingdon and New York: Routledge, 2018), pp. 263–274.

Chapter 3

The changing nature of school geography

How it began

The subject of geography has ancient origins. Indeed, many ancient philosophers would, in the modern world, find themselves working in a university's geography faculty. The word "geography" itself comes from Eratosthenes, writing in the second century BC, and means "writing the earth". This definition helps to see how these early approaches were largely concerned with describing different regions of the known world and recording the different phenomena which occurred there. This tradition of geographical study continued in the Arab world during the European Dark Ages before being embraced again in Europe during the Renaissance as various states became more interested in charting and studying the world to support their burgeoning ambitions of empire.

At this point there was something of a revolution in the subject. As a lecturer in geography at Königsberg, Immanuel Kant (better known for his wider philosophical writing) divided the subject into two, recognising a difference between the traditional approach that studied geography in terms of the earth's regions and a newer, more-scientific, thematic approach, which studied each phenomenon that shaped the earth in isolation (for a more detailed account of this difference, see Chapter 7). At this point we can also see a more scientific approach being taken to the study of regions, with a greater focus on gathering and analysing data. A recognisably geographical disciplinary approach had been born.

By the end of the 19th century and going into the 20th century, in England, the focus had shifted onto geography as a subject for the growing number of children now attending state schools to study. The subject's focus was on teaching children about the world through the prism of the British Empire – for example, about the colonies and the resources they supplied. Geography was not an academic discipline at this time, and was only established as one in order to supply geography graduates to teach the subject in schools. This makes geography unusual, with the school subject shaping the academic discipline, rather than the other way around.

Once established in universities, though, the subject took on a life of its own. Over the 20th century it fractured into various sub-disciplines, such as development studies and environmental policy, and increasingly developed into various "critical geographies", such as Marxist geographies or feminist geographies. The early link between school and academic geography continued well into the second half of the 20th century, with ideas from universities occasionally feeding into what was being taught in school, often via links to subject associations such as the Geographical Association and the Royal Geographical Society and through organisations such as the School's Council that ran ongoing training for teachers in areas like curriculum development. In 1988 all of this was to change.

The national curriculum and its evolution

The post-war years could be viewed as a golden age in terms of teacher autonomy over the curriculum in the UK.[1] There was no national curriculum to follow and very little in the way of accountability for educational outcomes. Whilst this could bring advantages if pupils were lucky enough to have a knowledgeable geography teacher, their experiences were patchy. This was particularly an issue in primary schools, where the pupils were at the mercy of their teacher's own interests.[2] A 1978 report from Her Majesty's Inspectors (HMI) reveals that the quality of work done in geography classrooms was often poor and had little sense of progression over time.[3] There were also concerns that the curriculum was overly dominated by what were seen as left-wing academic ideologies, ignoring the cultural transmission of knowledge that schools had originally been set up to deliver (we're back to Young's Future 1 vs Future 2 debate from Chapter 2).

These concerns eventually led to the Education Act of 1988, which paved the way for the first national curriculum in 1991. This curriculum was designed to overcome

---

1   John Hopkin and Fran Martin, Geography in the National Curriculum for Key Stages 1, 2 and 3. In Mark Jones and David Lambert (eds), *Debates in Geography Education*, 2nd edn (Abingdon and New York: Routledge, 2018), pp. 17–32.
2   Fran Martin, The place of knowledge in the new curriculum, *Primary Geography* 82(3) (2013): 9–11.
3   Department of Education and Science, *Primary Education in England: A Survey by HM Inspectors of Schools* (London: Her Majesty's Stationery Office, 1978). Available at: http://www.educationengland.org.uk/documents/hmi-primary/.

some of the perceived issues with the system in the preceding decades. It would ensure that all pupils in state schools received an education in the same subjects, covering the same content. Progression over the various key stages would be built in with clear assessment objectives and a focus on the transmission of an agreed body of knowledge. This first iteration of the national curriculum was therefore highly prescriptive and led to teachers being recast from curriculum *creators* (with a degree of autonomy over the content that is taught in the classroom) to curriculum *enactors* (with a degree of autonomy over *how* the content is taught in the classroom). However, in effect, teachers became curriculum *deliverers* (simply transferring the curriculum from the page to the pupil).[4] This was, at least in part, because the quantity of prescribed content was so vast that there was little time to do much more than attempt to get through everything as quickly as possible. As a result, the curriculum was slimmed down just a few years later, in 1995. Although the amount of content was reduced, the aims remained largely the same.

The national curriculum at Key Stage 3 has been reformed a further three times since then (and Key Stages 1 and 2 twice), twice by the Labour government that came into power in 1997 (the 2000 and the 2008 curriculum) and then again most recently by the Conservative-majority coalition government following their election in 2010 (the 2014 curriculum). These changes allow us to see the extent to which the national curriculum is a political document, and how this affects the teaching of geography in our schools.

The reforms in 2000 and 2008 led to a focus-shift away from the transmission of geographical knowledge and towards the prioritisation of the development of values and cross-curricular skills.[5] John Hopkin and Fran Martin illustrate this by highlighting how environmental issues have been approached across the Key Stage 3 national curriculum. In the original 1991 version there is a list of things that pupils are expected to know, such as the difference between renewable and non-renewable resources or how areas of scenic attraction can lead to competing

---

4   Mary Biddulph, Curriculum enactment. In Mark Jones and David Lambert (eds), *Debates in Geography Education*, 2nd edn (Abingdon and New York: Routledge, 2018), pp. 156–170.
5   Hopkin and Martin, Geography in the National Curriculum.

demands. By 2008 the prescribed content had gone and all that was left was the overarching issue that pupils must study, namely:

> interactions between people and their environments, including causes and consequences of these interactions, and how to plan for and manage their future impact.[6]

The content has been removed. The national curriculum no longer gives any indication of which interactions between people and environment should be studied or in which places. Instead, we are directed to spend our time on the much more generic skill of planning and managing future impacts.

Bill Marsden suggests that the shifts between subject knowledge transmission, wider educational orientation and social dimensions of education are part of a constant flux in schools.[7] Gert Biesta argues that this is because education is multidimensional and that schools must always balance the competing demands of qualification, socialisation and subjectification.[8] In his view, we can't *just* focus on qualification (transmitting knowledge, skills and dispositions) without initiating pupils into subject traditions (socialisation) or affecting their awareness of themselves in relation to that knowledge (subjectification). For example, we might teach a class about environmental issues, leading them to develop a greater knowledge and understanding of issues around sustainable development (qualification), become aware of society's desires for people to act more responsibly (socialisation) and then realise that they have the agency to enact these changes (subjectification).

Whilst it is possible to see that all three of Biesta's multidimensional educational purposes can co-exist, it is also difficult to ignore Marsden's point that there are shifts in terms of which purpose dominates at any one time in the national curriculum. We can see these shifts through a number of ways of categorising these different purposes, but I would argue there is a great deal of overlap.

6   Department for Children, Schools and Families and Qualifications and Curriculum Authority, *The National Curriculum: Statutory Requirements for Key Stages 3 and 4* (London: Department for Children, Schools and Families and Qualifications and Curriculum Authority, 2007), p. 106.
7   Bill Marsden, On taking the geography out of geographical education: some historical pointers, *Geography* 82(3) (1997): 241–252.
8   Biesta, What is education for?

Mary Biddulph proposes that there are three different perspectives on curriculum:[9]

- Cultural transmission (early 20th century and 1991 and 1995 national curriculum).

- Objectives-led (1970s/1980s and 2000 and 2008 national curriculum).

- Process and praxis.

John Hopkin proposes the following three perspectives on the geography curriculum in particular:[10]

- Traditional approach – the acquisition of objective facts about the world (early 20th century and 1991 and 1995 national curriculum).

- Global citizenship – links to other subjects and the development of skills and values (1970s/1980s and 2000 and 2008 national curriculum).

- Knowledgeable geography – recognising the merit of geographical knowledge and understanding based on core geographical ideas.

To these we could add Michael Young and Johan Muller's three futures model, as described in Chapter 2.[11]

- Future 1 – the transmission of knowledge as uncontested facts (early 20th century and 1991 and 1995 national curriculum).

- Future 2 – pupils facilitated to create their own understanding of the world and to develop desirable values (1970s/1980s and 2000 and 2008 national curriculum).

- Future 3 – pupils develop disciplinary knowledge.

Geography education over the 20th century and into the 21st has fluctuated, albeit slowly, between Future 1 and Future 2: knowledge transmission and values development. What we have not seen, at least not on a national scale, is a move towards Future 3 (as suggested by Young and Muller), process and praxis (as suggested by Biddulph) or knowledgeable geography (as suggested by Hopkin).

---

9 Mary Biddulph, What kind of curriculum do we really want?, *Teaching Geography* 39(1) (2014): 6–9.
10 John Hopkin, A "knowledgeable geography" approach to global learning, *Teaching Geography* 40(2) (2015): 50–54.
11 Young and Muller, Three educational scenarios for the future.

Where that leaves us

This movement between two poles, and the ignoring of a third approach, in school geography should not be surprising. There is something comforting about both Future 1 and Future 2 approaches to the national curriculum. With Future 1, we are given a body of knowledge to pass on to pupils. The fact that there is consistency in content means that resources can be created and shared between teachers and between schools, textbooks can be made, pedagogy can focus simply on how to teach in a way that makes this knowledge stick in the memory, at least until the next assessment. As professionals, this approach is relatively undemanding.

What Future 1 does rely on, however, is a certain amount of well-developed subject knowledge on the part of the teacher. To return to the example of the environmental issues listed in the 1991 national curriculum, you would need to know the difference between renewable and non-renewable resources and the characteristics of each. You would need to be confident in your knowledge of the problems surrounding competing demands in scenic areas and have examples to call upon. With Future 2, many of the demands placed upon your own subject knowledge are taken away. Your role as a teacher is not to transmit what you know about your subject, because all knowledge is socially constructed anyway, so what you know does not matter. Hopkin and Martin argue that teachers' insecurity about their own subject knowledge leads to problematic curricular decisions being taken:

> In the case of geography, there is evidence that this leads to a focus on contexts such as sustainable behaviours and skills such as enquiry, while content and concepts in the form of geographical knowledge and understanding may be underplayed or lost.[12]

If we feel we do not know enough about renewable resources or demands on scenic landscapes, then Future 2 provides some comfort. We can focus our energies on reaching vaguer objectives about pupils learning to respect the natural environment and changing their behaviour as a result. We can use lesson time to create posters about turning lights off when not in use or leaflets urging people to

12 Hopkin and Martin, Geography in the National Curriculum, p. 26.

look after the rainforests. This would also allow us to pay heed to calls from wider society to avoid teaching pupils *useless facts* and to fulfil wider societal aims, such as producing responsible citizens who are well versed in whichever issues are currently in vogue. This form of curriculum planning – responding to current events and concerns – also helps the teacher who is insecure in their own subject knowledge as they will be surrounded with at least surface-level information about the topics that they are going to cover.

That these two competing views on curriculum exist within the education system, jostling for dominance, creates a number of problems for us as teachers. Firstly, it affects our own conception of the curriculum, often narrowing our views down to these two poles. When the Conservative-led coalition government came into power in 2010 they were keen to signal that they would be making dramatic changes to the English education system. They felt that education was firmly rooted in a dominant Future 2 "progressive" tradition, and that this "Blob" – as the then secretary of state for education, Michael Gove, termed it – was a barrier to improving education through a move back towards a traditional, Future 1 approach to knowledge.[13] If they were right, then generations of teachers will have entered the profession steeped in one view of education and of the role of knowledge in the curriculum. These teachers will have been wary of knowledge transmission and seen their role as facilitators of learning, helping pupils to develop those values and character traits deemed valuable by society. There is evidence that this is indeed the case and can be seen in the reaction to the changes to the curriculum proposed by Gove and made manifest in the 2014 national curriculum.

Of course, the extent to which teachers are wedded to one particular view of the curriculum, *en masse*, is debatable. A modifying factor has always been the demands of the exam system, particularly in secondary schools. This does, however, highlight the second problem we face: the conflict inherent in the system. We can see some of the debates around the role of knowledge in the curriculum played out in the geography GCSE specifications and exams, with perhaps a greater focus on pupils applying their own ideas to geographical issues in a Future 2 model, but some transmission of knowledge has always been necessary for pupils to succeed. This, then, puts teachers in something of a bind. We have the whole apparatus of teacher development – from initial teacher training (ITT) to

---

13 Richard Garner, What is "the Blob" and why is Michael Gove comparing his enemies to an unbeatable sci-fi mound of goo which once battled Steve McQueen?, *The Independent* (7 February 2014). Available at: https://www.independent.co.uk/news/education/education-news/what-is-the-blob-and-why-is-michael-gove-comparing-his-enemies-to-an-unbeatable-sci-fi-mound-of-goo-9115600.html.

continuing professional development (CPD) – focusing on an approach that downplays the transmission of knowledge in the curriculum but an exam and accountability system in which the transmission of knowledge is necessary. It is hardly any wonder that we end up with a confused system and a confused curriculum.

I would argue that the break between Key Stages 1–3 and Key Stages 4–5 has also encouraged us to see the exam specifications as a de facto curriculum. A Future 2 approach is encouraged in the earlier key stages, but external exams mean that teachers have felt forced into a Future 1 style transmission of a given body of knowledge, wherein the purpose of education is to ensure that as much of the content specified by the exam board is retained by the pupil – and for long enough – to do well in the exam. Because we, as a profession, have been so wary of the transmission of knowledge, we have not had a conversation about how qualifications could be approached in a different way: a way that leads to powerful knowledge of geography, which just so happens to also allow pupils to excel in exams. What this would need is a focus on that third perspective on curriculum – articulated variously by Biddulph, Hopkin, and Muller and Young – and would involve us all keeping our subject discipline central to the curriculum. Unfortunately, as I'll show in the next chapter, we have lost sight of our subject.

Questions

- To what extent do you feel that a teacher's own subject knowledge might be a barrier to delivering a powerful geography curriculum?

- In your experience, is there is a difference in approach to subjects that are being examined externally (through GCSEs and SATs) compared with those that are not (such as foundation subjects at Key Stage 2 or geography at Key Stage 3)?

- Reviewing the most recent national curriculum, do you feel it fits more into a Future 1 or Future 2 view of knowledge?

Further reading

Mary Biddulph, What do we mean by curriculum? In Mark Jones (ed.), *The Handbook of Secondary Geography* (Sheffield: The Geographical Association, 2017), pp. 30–39.

John Hopkin and Fran Martin, Geography in the National Curriculum for Key Stages 1, 2 and 3. In Mark Jones and David Lambert (eds), *Debates in Geography Education*, 2nd edn (Abingdon and New York: Routledge, 2018), pp. 17–32.

Chapter 4

Losing sight of the subject

Breaking down divides between subjects

As we have seen, a central tenet of Michael Young's idea of powerful knowledge is that it is created by academic disciplines in their own distinct search for truth and, therefore, this knowledge needs to be taught as distinct subjects in schools. However, over the years there has been a push to move away from organising the school day along traditional subject lines. Some critics point to the fact that modern school timetables look remarkably like the list of subjects introduced by the newly formed Board of Education in their secondary school regulations, published in 1904. They say of the curriculum:

> The course should provide for instruction in the English language and literature, at least one language other than English, geography, history, mathematics, science and drawing, with due provision for manual work and physical exercises; and, in a girls' school, for housewifery. Not less than 4½ hours per week must be allotted to English, geography and history; not less than 3½ hours to the language where only one is taken or less than 6 hours where two are taken; and not less than 7½ hours to science and mathematics, of which at least 3 must be for science. The instruction in science must be both theoretical and practical. Where two languages other than English are taken, and Latin is not one of them, the Board will require to be satisfied that the omission of Latin is for the advantage of the school.[1]

With the exception of housewifery and Latin the only real change is the addition of a few other subjects such as computer science and personal, social, health and

---

1 Board of Education, *Regulations for Secondary Schools* (1904). Available at: http://www.educationengland. org.uk/documents/boardofed/1904-secondary-regulations.html.

economic (PSHE) education. This has led to calls for change, with the assumption that a curriculum designed for 1904 cannot possibly be relevant today.

One of the changes that is often proposed is to remove the barriers between subjects and to instead teach through cross-curricular synoptic projects. One of the most well-known attempts to bring this approach into schools is the RSA Opening Minds project, which suggests organising the curriculum around five key competencies:

1   Citizenship

2   Learning

3   Managing Information

4   Relating to People

5   Managing Situations[2]

These competencies are approached through lessons that cut across traditional subject divides. They state:

> Some commentators argue that a competency based approach is in opposition to the acquisition of subject knowledge. That is a misunderstanding about the nature of Opening Minds: it is not an alternative to the teaching of subject knowledge – rather it is an alternative way of delivering it.[3]

However, we can see that the aim is not the development of subject knowledge itself, but of the wider competencies that this knowledge will enable – many of which, such as Managing Information, the RSA aim to achieve through the model of delivery rather than the content. This stands in stark opposition to the notion of powerful knowledge, in which the content itself is the enabler.

Although few schools adopted the kind of radical approaches put forward by RSA Opening Minds and others, the idea of developing generic competencies *within* subject lessons became common during the Future 2 period of curriculum

2   See http://www.rsaopeningminds.org.uk/about-rsa-openingminds/.
3   See http://www.rsaopeningminds.org.uk/about-rsa-openingminds/opening-minds-and-the-national-curiculum/.

thinking. This perhaps reached its apotheosis in the 2007 national curriculum for England, which presented the following three aims:

The curriculum should enable all young people to become:

- *successful learners who enjoy learning, make progress and achieve*
- *confident individuals who are able to live safe, healthy and fulfilling lives*
- *responsible citizens who make a positive contribution to society.*[4]

Each of these broad aims was then divided down further. For example, confident individuals:

- have a sense of self-worth and personal identity
- relate well to others and form good relationships
- are self-aware and deal well with their emotions
- have secure values and beliefs, and have principles to distinguish right from wrong
- become increasingly independent, are able to take the initiative and organise themselves
- make healthy lifestyle choices
- are physically competent and confident
- take managed risks and stay safe
- recognise their talents and have ambitions
- are willing to try new things and make the most of opportunities
- are open to the excitement and inspiration offered by the natural world and human achievements.[5]

---

4   Department for Children, Schools and Families and Qualifications and Curriculum Authority, *The National Curriculum*, p. 7.
5   Department for Children, Schools and Families and Qualifications and Curriculum Authority, *The National Curriculum*, p. 7.

The idea was for these aims to be reflected in the curriculum areas for each subject or sought through cross-curricular projects. The actual prescribed content for geography was almost non-existent. The expectation for learning about physical and human processes was described as:

> Understanding how sequences of events and activities in the physical and human worlds lead to change in places, landscapes and societies.[6]

I think we can contrast the long list of generic aims with the sparse and undefined subject content in the curriculum and see where schools' priorities were directed. A geography lesson was just as likely to focus on an attempt to help pupils relate well to others and form good relationships as teach them about the drivers of migration or the formation of coastal landforms. This, of course, suited a Future 2 conception of knowledge in the curriculum, in which knowledge is subjective and cannot be passed from one person to another, but also fitted with the growing fear that technology was making subject-specific knowledge redundant in a world in which pupils could "just google it".

In her book *Seven Myths About Education*, Daisy Christodoulou tackles the idea that modern technology makes the learning of factual, declarative knowledge redundant.[7] She cites the likes of Don Tapscott, who argued in 2008 that:

> Teachers are no longer the fountain of knowledge; the internet is ... They can look that up and position it in history with a click on Google.[8]

and Jon Overton, who claimed that:

> We are no longer in an age where a substantial "fact bank" in our heads is required.[9]

---

6 Department for Children, Schools and Families and Qualifications and Curriculum Authority, *The National Curriculum*, p. 103.
7 Daisy Christodoulou, *Seven Myths About Education* (Abingdon and New York: Routledge, 2014).
8 Alexandra Frean, Google generation has no need for rote learning, *The Times* (2 December 2008).
9 ATL, *Report: The Magazine from the Association of Teachers and Lecturers* (May 2012), p. 14. Available at: https://issuu.com/atlunion/docs/report-may-2012.

She also discusses proposals from RSA Opening Minds and from the educational charity Futurelab, which argued for schools to move away from teaching pupils facts and, instead, teach them where to find these facts for themselves and how to evaluate them for accuracy and bias. She also shows that this style of education was, at the time, preferred by accountability body Ofsted. There seems to be ample evidence to assert that there is a pressure to move away from the teaching of geography in the geography classroom, instead focusing on pupils' generic competency in using technology to access the geography for themselves.

However, as Christodoulou shows, the idea that we can outsource our knowledge to the internet is a myth. Our ability to find – and, more importantly, understand – new information is based on what we already know. Our working memories are limited to just a few pieces of new information. If we need to look up everything we want to know, we have to hold it all in our head before we can think about it and try to reach some kind of conclusion. As an example, let's say we want to think about the Lesotho Highlands Water Project and whether it was a sustainable development for southern Africa. To make this decision, we would, at the very least, need the following pieces of declarative knowledge:

- The location of Lesotho and its neighbour.
- The details of the project – economic cost, social cost, environmental impact, etc.
- The meaning of the concept of *sustainability*.
- The views of different stakeholders.
- The climate patterns of the region and the role of the mountains.

Knowing each of these things would also be predicated on knowing other things. For example, the views of different stakeholders:

- The nature of farming in low-income countries.
- The water demands of industry.
- Water availability in informal settlements.

Whilst it might be possible to look up each of these things, and then everything you didn't understand about what you had just looked up, the demand on your limited working memory would be enormous. If we want pupils to understand the world, they need to *know* about the world. It is not enough to just know that this knowledge is out there somewhere. If we want to use it, we have to own it.

The geography of good intentions

With geography being taken out of the geography curriculum there was a vacuum that needed to be filled. As Alex Standish explains:

> **Indeed, it is the failure of teachers to communicate to students the importance of knowledge to human society that has led to the infusion of moral values into the curriculum.**[10]

Without a focus on geographical knowledge, the focus has to go elsewhere. Luckily – or unluckily, depending on your view – there has never been a shortage of people with ideas about what should be taught via geography lessons. After all, if *anything* is geography, anything can be placed in your curriculum. As Standish explains, the New Labour curriculum reforms of the early 2000s were less prescriptive in terms of subject content, whilst the agenda for citizenship and education for sustainable development became more visible in both policy and practice.

It has to be remembered that this is not only a problem of this millennium. Bill Marsden explains that there are three components of curriculum planning that need to be kept in balance and that problems arise when any one of them dominates.[11] He identifies them as:

- *the subject component* in which the recall of content dominates (which we could think of as Future 1)

- *the educational component* in which relatively content-free cross-curricular projects dominate (Future 2, such as the RSA Opening Minds project)

- *the social component* in which there is a focus on contemporary causes.

10 Alex Standish, Valuing (adult) geographic knowledge, *Geography* 89(1) (2004): 89–91 at 89.
11 Marsden, On taking the geography out of geographical education.

Marsden, writing in 1997, suggests that this social component could be seen as dominant in the geography curricula of individual schools of the 1960s and 1970s. He issues a warning:

> that dominance of the educational and/or social education components will tend to drive the geography out of geographical education [...] Furthermore, the historical record suggests that where social and/or ideological objectives are given primacy, there is a high risk of politicisation of the curriculum, and of the justification of instruction.[12]

He points to the work of Sir Archibald Geikie, in the late 19th century, who espoused a progressive and child-centred view of education in which a child's interests could drive the geography curriculum. He also favoured a highly instructional approach when it came to ensuring that they behaved towards the environment in a way in which he felt was correct.

One of the most influential figures in the creation of school geography was Sir Halford Mackinder, an academic and author of many early geography textbooks. Although he was highly critical of some of Geikie's ideas about what constituted suitable topics for inclusion in the geography curriculum, he was in favour of using it to shape the ideas and attitudes of schoolchildren. In Mackinder's case this was towards a pro-imperialist position: shaping children as supporters of the British Empire. This continued into the 20th century, and in the inter-war years we saw the introduction of what would now be called "fundamental British values" to the curriculum, with the aim of inducing patriotism in the nation's young. Other forces argued that the geography curriculum should instead be used to show how places were interconnected and to help young people imagine the lives of others and so develop empathy. Either way, the curriculum was moving beyond ensuring that children had knowledge with which to think and skipping straight to what those in power wanted them to think. As Alex Standish wrote:

> Examination questions on ethical issues began to appear on GCSE articles – and these were short-answer questions, where there is no room to develop an argument.[13]

12 Marsden, On taking the geography out of geographical education, 242.
13 Alex Standish, Constructing a value map, *Geography* 88(2) (2003): 149–151 at 149.

Pupils simply needed to provide the *correct* ethical answer. As Marsden puts it, "good causes tend to generate inculcation and indoctrination rather than genuine education."[14] He concludes that, as a result of this, not only the *geography* but also the *education* was taken out of geography education.

Although Marsden was writing about these problems in 1997 – and looking back to the 1960s, 1970s and beyond – we can see an echo in the reforms that followed a decade later and resulted in the geography curriculum in many schools being subjected to the sways of popular concerns. Issues around knife crime could be addressed through geography of crime units, single-use plastics in a topic on the oceans, or climate change as a stand-alone topic or taught through its impact on other areas of geography.

This might have been less of an issue if these topics were to be explored geographically. The use of resources, including plastics and their impacts, is an important geographical topic, as is the ways in which crime impacts different groups of people in a community. However, if we take the view that the geographical knowledge is unimportant, the purpose becomes convincing pupils to behave in a certain way or take action over the issue. Although well-meaning, this creates a range of problems:

- It tends to ignore the geographical complexity of the issue. A geographer looking at single-use plastics would want to weigh up the problems with this material against its advantages, such as its ability to preserve food for longer. Any claim about the environmental problems of using a resource would need to consider this complexity. This is missed if we only teach it as an "issue".

- History tells us that it does not work. Schools have been trying this approach for decades. If it made a difference to behaviour, we would have a generation of people in their forties who refuse to drive and recycle religiously, and we would have regenerated the world's rainforests. This has not happened.

- It lets those with the power to create change off the hook. If we accept that it is schools' responsibility to solve these problems through the curriculum, then we are also accepting that nothing is going to change until our pupils reach an age when they have the agency to enact change. In the meantime,

14 Marsden, On taking the geography out of geographical education, 244.

those who *could* do something about it now can just pass the blame onto schools for not teaching about the issues.

- Knowledgeable people are best placed to deal with society's problems. If we really want to deal with these kinds of issues, then we need people who possess the powerful knowledge to solve them. The problems around single-use plastics are not going to be solved by those who can design a compelling leaflet, but by people with excellent disciplinary knowledge on environmental geography and resource management. When we push knowledge off the curriculum to make space for a more generic look at an issue, we paradoxically make it harder to solve the issue in the future.

The power of curriculum creation

Throughout the first half of the 20th century there was a constant dialogue between academic geographers (those who created new geographical knowledge) and geography teachers and educationalists (those who recontextualised this knowledge for the classroom). As Marsden points out, during the 1950s the Geographical Association had 14 academic geographers as presidents and three teachers. At no point was it headed by someone from a more general educationalist background. Likewise, their journal, *Geography*, was edited by professors of geography. Academic geography continued to have a major influence on the school curriculum via the Geographical Association and as a result of members also writing school textbooks.[15]

Up to, and including, the 1950s we can see the subject component dominating school geography, possibly at the expense of the educational and social components. This was to change in the 1960s and 1970s with curriculum theories entering the discussion and then teacher training programmes, and critical theories on the subject entering academic geography and shaping the subject itself to be more aware of, and concerned with, a range of social issues. It is possible that at this point a balance was being found between these three different components of curriculum purpose.

---

15 Marsden, On taking the geography out of geographical education, 245–246.

Unfortunately, it seems as though what looked like balance was just the bottom of the arc as the pendulum swung away from the subject component. Since 1973 no academic geographer has held the role of president of the Geographical Association. The final academic geographer to hold the role, Andrew Goudie, had the following warning to give in 1993:

> for the most part the current generation of academics choose not to serve on GA committees or its Council, they do not join the Association, they choose not to send their best articles to its journals, and few attend its Annual Conference. A chasm has developed between those who teach at school and those who teach in universities.[16]

From the 1970s onwards there was an increasing influence from the new field of curriculum studies, which was pushing for a more integrated approach to the curriculum, with a breaking down of subject barriers and a focus on the way in which subjects such as geography could shape young people's attitudes. The curriculum at this time was heavily focused on process rather than content, and there was a growing unease in political circles that this was leading to it being dumbed down, with too little rigour in terms of what was being learnt. These concerns culminated in the introduction of England's first national curriculum – to be taught from 1991 – which focused heavily on the content to be learnt before being followed in the 2000s by a national curriculum that focused on process and those generic aims discussed at the start of this chapter. One problem was that political control over the content of the first national curriculum took the decisions over what geography to teach away from the teachers. When later iterations of the national curriculum removed this content, there was nothing to replace it. This led to a focus in schools on *how* things were learnt rather than *what* was being learnt. As Clare Brooks has pointed out:

> the emphasis on lesson planning as a technical task can mean that this reflection is directed at the pedagogical success of the lesson. Were the students engaged? Was the task successful and completed? Did the students meet the lesson objectives?[17]

16 Andrew Goudie, Schools and universities – the great divide, *Geography* 78(4) (1993): 338–339 at 338–339.
17 Clare Brooks, Geography teachers and making the school geography curriculum, *Geography* 91(1) (2006): 75–83 at 82.

She suggests that these are not the only questions we should be asking and that we also need to ask:

> Are we teaching good geography? Are our representations of other places fair and balanced? Do our lessons enable students to appreciate the complexity of the world and the underlying mechanisms that shape and affect the world that we live in? Was the content of the resource used appropriate for this geographical issue?[18]

In the words of Bill Marsden, we have taken the geography out of geography education.

Through this brief look at the history of our subject we can see a shift in the ownership of curriculum creation from academic geographers, through educationalists, to politicians. What has often been missing from this struggle for control is the voice of classroom teachers. In the next chapter I will suggest that this is about to change as we rise up and take power through a manifesto for a powerful geography curriculum.

Questions

- To what extent do you feel that digital technology changes the need to teach declarative knowledge?
- Can you think of occasions when a curriculum you have taught has focused more on good intentions than on the teaching of geography?
- Reviewing your curriculum, are there any topics in which you can see a lack of geographical knowledge?

18 Brooks, Geography teachers and making the school geography curriculum, 82.

Further reading

Alex Standish, *Global Perspectives in the Geography Curriculum: Reviewing the Moral Case for Geography* (Abingdon and New York: Routledge, 2009).

David Lambert, Thinking geographically. In Mark Jones (ed.), *The Handbook of Secondary Geography* (Sheffield: The Geographical Association, 2017), pp. 20–29.

Chapter 5
Finding our way again

Future 3 curriculum

The curriculum that our pupils experience is created at a number of different levels. We have national guidelines provided by the government or their agencies which, in turn, is shaped by the advice offered by subject associations and through the resources that are created to help teach the content. This is then developed further by individual schools, departments and teachers who turn this into a (hopefully) coherent whole for their pupils. As Clare Brooks concludes, quoting the Curriculum Development Working Group of the Department for Education and Skills Geography Focus Group (2005):

> **The phrase "curriculum-making" therefore reflects "the curriculum which is experienced by students and made by teachers in school".[1]**

It is the teacher who, finally, *makes* the curriculum. However, in the past these decisions have often been dictated to a high degree: by those in academia setting the tone for what they felt should constitute school geography and to what end (such as cultivating support for the British Empire or developing patriotism), by competency-based curricula that insisted the subject take a back seat to generic skills, or through the inclusion of so much prescribed content that the teacher was left with little opportunity to do more than race through it.

---

1   Brooks, Geography teachers and making the school geography curriculum, 77.

Writing about the most recent national curriculum, Eleanor Rawling argues that:

> Despite later changes to the geography NC that allowed greater recognition of concepts and scope for professional input, the 2013 review reinstated what seemed to be a static "list-of-content" curriculum.[2]

Her concern here is that this prevents teachers from having the agency to meaningfully "make" the curriculum in their classrooms. However, in Chapter 6 I will suggest that the latest curriculum for Key Stages 1–3 is remarkably light on content prescription, giving only broad topics and places that must be taught but no sense of the depth of coverage needed. This gives teachers remarkable freedom in deciding what should be taught, how and to what end. For example, the Key Stage 2 curriculum states that "rivers" should be taught. However, it does not say whether this should involve pupils knowing how every landform is created and changes over time, the causes and management of floods or simply the processes carried out by a river. It will be the school and, ultimately, the teacher in the classroom who decides what their intention is when teaching "rivers".

With the removal of generic competencies from the national curriculum and the paring down of prescriptive content we as teachers now hold the balance of power in making the curriculum an opportunity to move beyond the Future 1 recall of facts and Future 2 rejection of subject knowledge and towards a Future 3 in which we focus on developing an understanding of the world through geographical disciplinary knowledge in all its forms.

In order to achieve this aim, we first need to identify what we mean by *geographical knowledge* as distinct from *anything is geography*. This is an area in which geography often runs into difficulties as it is such a broad domain, covering everything from development studies to soil horizons to environmental policy. Finding the threads that join these seemingly disparate topics together is not easy, but that has not stopped us from trying. Liz Taylor compiled a number of examples of geographer's attempts to classify the big ideas underpinning geography for various reasons.[3] Even a cursory glance reveals that there is little agreement beyond "space", "place" and "scale" that appear in most, although not all, lists. For example, Sarah Holloway et al., in creating a reader for undergraduate study, add:

2   Eleanor Rawling, How and why national curriculum frameworks are failing geography, *Geography* 105(2) (2020): 69–77.
3   Liz Taylor, Key concepts and medium term planning, *Teaching Geography* 33(2) (2008): 50–54.

- Social formations
- Physical systems
- Landscape and environment[4]

Whereas David Leat misses "space", "place" and "environment" completely in favour of:

- Cause and effect
- Classification
- Decision-Making
- Development
- Inequality
- Location
- Planning Systems[5]

Taylor suggests that what we see in such lists is a difference between substantive concepts (the content) and the second-order concepts which are "the ideas used to organise the content and to shape questions within a discipline."[6] She adds the following suggestions as second-order concepts in geography:

- Diversity
- Change
- Interaction
- Perception and representation[7]

4   Sarah Holloway, Stephen Rice and Gill Valentine (eds), *Key Concepts in Geography*, 1st edn (London: Sage, 2003).
5   David Leat, The importance of "big" concepts and skills in learning geography. In Chris Fisher and Tony Binns (eds), *Issues in Geography Teaching* (London and New York: RoutledgeFalmer, 2000), pp. 137–151.
6   Taylor, Key concepts and medium term planning, 54.
7   Taylor, Key concepts and medium term planning.

As well as there being little agreement on the exact big ideas that make geography a *unified* discipline, there is also an issue with identifying what makes it a *distinct* discipline. Many of the big ideas compiled by Taylor could just as easily be claimed by other subjects. For example, Holloway et al.'s social formations could apply to sociology and Leat's cause and effect and classification by the sciences.

David Lambert suggests that we can best see how geography is a specialised discipline in its language and grammar.[8] The language is the content that is taught – the substantive knowledge – whereas the grammar is the distinctly geographical way in which this content is approached. This grammar, then, is comprised of the concepts and theories that help us make sense of the world in a way that leaves us thinking geographically – the disciplinary knowledge. On top of this we have the distinctive way in which geographers use procedural knowledge to investigate the world; not the maps and graphs themselves (which are used by a range of disciplines) but the way in which they are put to use. The powerful geography we seek to teach is therefore the language and grammar of geography. Through this our pupils will be able to experience the world geographically, think geographically, and describe their experiences and express their thoughts in a geographical way. They will be writing the world.

Peter Jackson reflects on Lambert's idea and proposes his own list of geography's distinctive big ideas that provide the grammar for our subject. These are:

- Space and place
- Scale and connection
- Proximity and distance
- Relational thinking[9]

Jackson then shows how these big ideas could apply to thinking geographically about the seemingly simple decision about whether to buy a goat for someone living in a low-income country. He explains that thinking about proximity and distance can give us an understanding of the ease with which we give money to people in other parts of the world compared with the relative difficulty of taking

8   David Lambert, The Power of Geography (2004). Available at: https://www.geography.org.uk/write/MediaUploads/Advocacy%20Files/NPOGPower.doc.

9   Peter Jackson, Thinking geographically, *Geography* 91(3) (2006): 199–204.

action to address inequalities in our own neighbourhoods. Alternatively, a knowledge and understanding of connection can allow us to understand the risk of desertification posed by goat husbandry, and the cycle of poverty this can create. These big ideas therefore move us beyond the simplistic geography of good intentions and towards an ability to think geographically about the complexity of the world.

David Lambert and John Morgan suggest that simply identifying this language and grammar – the powerful knowledge – is not enough. They argue that those making the curriculum also need to take into account pupils' experiences and how they will receive and respond to this powerful knowledge, as well as the teachers' choices as they recontextualise this powerful knowledge into a form that can be grasped by their pupils using appropriate pedagogies. They suggest that we can see this as a Venn diagram with pupils' experiences, teachers' choices and school geography overlapping.[10] Richard Bustin adapts this model and shows that in the centre of this diagram sits powerful knowledge, which can be identified by asking the following questions:

- Does this take the learner beyond what they already know?
- Which learning activity should be used?
- Is this underpinned by key concepts?
- Are they thinking geographically?[11]

Margaret Roberts makes the point that the teacher's choices are critical in making a powerful curriculum, arguing that:

> **Although geography has distinct and powerful ways of looking at the world, this does not answer the crucial curriculum question of exactly what to teach.[12]**

---

10 David Lambert and John Morgan, *Teaching Geography 11–18: A Conceptual Approach* (Maidenhead: Open University Press, 2010), p. 50.
11 Richard Bustin, *Geography Education's Potential and the Capabilities Approach: GeoCapabilities and Schools* (Cham: Palgrave Macmillan, 2019), p. 90.
12 Margaret Roberts, Powerful knowledge and geographical education, *The Curriculum Journal* 25(2) (2014): 187–209 at 203.

She goes on to give the example of the choices around the study of urban areas and suggests a whole range of things a teacher will have to consider when deciding what to study:

- Models of urban growth.

- Ethical issues around inequalities.

- Political factors that lead to decisions over urban change.

- The connections between urban areas and other places.

- Whether facts from specific case studies should be used and whether pupils should remember them all.

These are the kinds of questions that every teacher needs to be able to answer about their own curriculum and are the kinds of discussions that should be taking place in department meetings. They are also the kinds of questions discussed in Part II of this book, as we look to put the theory into practice.

Roberts is also clear that there needs to be a discussion about the pedagogy chosen by the teacher, pointing out that any curriculum is potentially powerful but is inert until it is brought to life in the minds of the pupils. Disciplinary knowledge cannot, she asserts, be transmitted to the pupils' minds from the teacher's but requires the pupils to engage with this knowledge. They need to enquire about geographical knowledge so that they can make sense of the way in which geographers ask questions, collect and analyse data, and reach conclusions.[13] Therefore the pedagogies chosen by the teacher are an important curriculum consideration. If we want to create a powerful geography curriculum we cannot teach in a way that presents knowledge as a list of facts to be learnt outside of any context (Future 1), but nor can we teach as though the recall of facts is trivial and unimportant (Future 2). In our Future 3 curriculum we teach in a way that ensures that pupils can recall facts, but we do it so that they can make use of them in the future and apply them to new scenarios. We are increasing their capabilities through this powerful knowledge.

---

13 Roberts, Powerful knowledge and geographical education, 204–205.

GeoCapabilities

The idea of capabilities in this context goes back to Nobel Prize winning economist Amartya Sen, who was concerned with developing a model for measuring the actual well-being of people. He argued that the simple measure of access to resources did not equal the same *functioning* for different people. For example, those with mobility issues might need greater access to technology to access the same functions as those without (such as mobility scooters or automatic doors); pregnant women might have different dietary requirements to those who are not pregnant to achieve the same functioning in their health (such as foods enriched with folic acid).[14] As Ingrid Robeyns explains it:

Functionings are thus outcomes or achievements, whereas capabilities are the real opportunities to achieve valuable states of being and doing.[15]

Sen therefore focused on capabilities and how they could be increased. It is important to note that this model is concerned with people having the capabilities to act as they want to, not with coercion to act in a certain way. This becomes important when considering its relevance to education and the curriculum.

Sen's work on capabilities views the purpose of education not through a purely utilitarian lens – through which schools are desirable only if they lead to particular outcomes (often measured in terms of improving the economy) – but from a position in which they are justified simply because they give the next generation the capabilities to do with as they wish. It fits with a view of education as an entitlement and therefore seems to align with Michael Young's view of children's entitlement to powerful knowledge as a social justice issue. Sen does not give a definitive list of capabilities, just as Young doesn't offer one for powerful knowledge, but others have tried to fill the gap. Richard Bustin gives a selection of these lists, and whilst there is some commonality – such as "life" and "health" – there are also many that only appear on one commentator's list and not others' – such as "art" and "enlightenment".[16] The list of capabilities that has been the most

---

14 Amartya Sen, Development as capability expansion, *Journal of Development Planning* 19 (1989): 41–58.
15 Ingrid Robeyns, Three models of education: rights, capabilities and human capital, *Theory and Research in Education* 4(1) (2006): 69–84 at 78.
16 Bustin, *Geography Education's Potential and the Capabilities Approach*, p. 104.

influential is that created by Martha Nussbaum, who was writing from a social justice perspective and with a particular focus on gender. She suggests the following list of capabilities "can be convincingly argued to be of central importance in any human life, whatever else the person pursues or chooses".[17]

- Life – not dying prematurely.

- Bodily health – having good health, including reproductive health.

- Bodily integrity – being able to move freely from place to place without the threat of violence.

- Sense, imagination and thought – being able to think and imagine freely and express oneself freely.

- Emotions – being able to feel freely and not to have our emotions only governed by fear.

- Practical reason – being able to think and reason about one's own life and choices.

- Affiliation – being able to live with others and to be treated with respect and without bias.

- Other species – living with our environment and treating it with concern.

- Play – being able to enjoy leisure time.

- Control over our environment – being able to take part in political choices and being able to hold property and have equal rights to employment.

Even this list has attracted criticism as offering a white, North American, middle class view of what everyone in the world should see as capabilities leading to desirable functionings.[18] Much like with powerful knowledge, as soon as someone tries to pin it down as a definitive list, it becomes open for debate. However, having this debate as professionals in charge of making the curriculum is an important process. We can start to ask, what capabilities do we think our young people are entitled to? The next question is, how will a curriculum rich in powerful geographical knowledge help to develop these capabilities?

17 Martha C. Nussbaum, *Women and Human Development: The Capabilities Approach* (Cambridge: Cambridge University Press, 2000), p. 74.
18 Bustin, *Geography Education's Potential and the Capabilities Approach*, p. 106.

There can be a temptation to see the capabilities approach to education through a Future 2 lens of generic competencies. If we want to develop the capacity to engage in political discussions we should just give pupils opportunities to discuss politics, and if we want them to have the capacity to use their senses to imagine we should just spend lots of time imagining things. However, as Bustin writes:

> **It is subject knowledge that enables young people to engage in debates and discussions, to think in new ways, to discern fact from fiction ...[19]**

When we look at these capabilities more deeply, we can see a strong role for powerful knowledge and a Future 3 curriculum.

There have been efforts to bring together the concepts of powerful knowledge and capabilities in a movement known as GeoCapabilities. This was first proposed by David Lambert and John Morgan,[20] and developed further by David Lambert, Michael Solem and Sirpa Tani[21] and, more recently, by Richard Bustin. As Bustin explains, it is:

> **an expression of how powerful geographical knowledge can enable children to think and behave in ways that promote freedoms in life. It articulates what studying geography attempts to achieve that no other subject can.[22]**

Lambert and Morgan did not originally provide a list of GeoCapabilities when writing about the theoretical concept. However, working with Solem and Tani, Lambert proposed such a list, including things like "promoting individual autonomy and freedom".[23] However, as Bustin points out, these are not distinctly geographical in nature. Any subject could claim this as a capability it is promoting.

---

19 Bustin, *Geography Education's Potential and the Capabilities Approach*, p. 116.
20 Lambert and Morgan, *Teaching Geography 11–18*.
21 David Lambert, Michael Solem and Sirpa Tani, Achieving human potential through geography education: a capabilities approach to curriculum making in schools, *Annals of the Association of American Geographers* 105(4) (2015): 723–735.
22 Bustin, *Geography Education's Potential and the Capabilities Approach*, p. 120.
23 Michael Solem, David Lambert and Sirpa Tani, Geocapabilities: toward an international framework for researching the purposes and values of geography education, *Review of International Geographical Education* 3(3) (2013): 214–229. Available at: http://www.rigeo.org/vol3no3/RIGEO-V3-N3-1.pdf.

What has far greater potential is the combination of Maude's work on powerful knowledge and Lambert's work on capabilities. This results in the following three distinctive GeoCapabilities, as discussed by Bustin:

1   The acquisition of deep descriptive and explanatory "world knowledge".

2   The development of relational thinking that underpins geographical thought.

3   A propensity to apply the analysis of alternative social, economic and environmental futures to particular place contexts.

Richard Bustin's book *Geography Education's Potential and the Capabilities Approach* gives a detailed breakdown of these three capabilities and provides a powerful description of what school geography could be. Acquiring world knowledge does not simply mean learning a list of capital cities – the "capes and bays" approach to the curriculum – but involves the teacher revealing the world to their pupils "through the way they frame and recontextualize knowledge".[24] As Bustin explains, no other subject does this. They may use places in a superficial way to locate some other knowledge, but they are not involving their classes in a deep exploration of those locations. The second capability seems to build on Jackson's big ideas for geography. It involves thinking of the world in terms of the processes that shape it and how one process may affect another. This detailed systems thinking is also distinctly geographical in nature. If pupils do not learn it with us, they are unlikely to learn this mode of thinking elsewhere. The third capability involves pupils thinking about potential futures. This means that they need to apply what they have learnt in geography to new scenarios in order to make predictions about changes that could occur at a range of scales (from erosion of a cliff to the evolving characteristics of a city or the changes that will arise from a warming climate).

Finding our purpose

In Part I of this book I have suggested that we – as a profession in general but as geography teachers in particular – have lost our way somewhat. Or, rather, that we have been led off track, following good intentions and bright promises. As a result it can be hard to articulate the purpose of our subject, and therefore of our curriculum, and we end up falling back on claims that "anything" is geography or trying

24 Bustin, *Geography Education's Potential and the Capabilities Approach*, p. 122.

to justify teaching geography through its ability to develop generic soft skills. The logical endpoint of this argument is that we don't need to teach geography at all, and we take the geography out of geography education, something that specialists – from Mackinder to Marsden, a hundred years apart – have been warning us against.

It has, however, been heartening to see a shift between 2010 and 2020 and a re-establishing of *geography* as the purpose of a geography curriculum. An assertion that teaching geography is a good thing in its own right, regardless of the outcomes it may lead to. I believe that this shift has occurred in part due to the work done by Michael Young on powerful knowledge and the focus given to this concept, first by David Lambert and then by the likes of Alaric Maude and, most recently, Richard Bustin. Seemingly unique to geography education has been the linking of powerful knowledge to Sen's capabilities approach to create GeoCapabilities.

Putting all of this together allows us to articulate a powerful purpose for the geography curriculum:

- Schools *can* serve many functions, but their *purpose* is to provide that which cannot be provided elsewhere.

- Schools should be gardens of peace, where children are given the *gift of teaching* – away from the concerns of wider society.

- Academic disciplines create knowledge in distinctive ways. By teaching pupils this disciplinary knowledge, we not only give them access to a vast repository of knowledge from previous generations but also teach them to see the world in distinctive ways.

- In geography, these distinctive big ideas include:[25]

  > Space and place.

  > Scale and connection.

  > Proximity and distance.

  > Relational thinking.

---

25 Jackson, Thinking geographically, 199.

- Teaching geography should give pupils the capability to:[26]

  > Discover new ways of thinking.

  > Better explain and understand the natural and social worlds.

  > Think about alternative futures and what they could do to influence them.

  > Have some power over their own knowledge.

  > Be able to engage in current debates of significance.

  > Go beyond the limits of their personal experience.

Part II of this book will look at how we put this purpose into practice in creating a powerful geography curriculum.

Questions

- What do you see as the *big ideas* in geography and how are these reflected in your curriculum?

- What capabilities do you think geography should cultivate in your pupils? How do you ensure that your curriculum achieves this?

- After reading Part I of this book, do you agree with the purpose outlined here? Why (or why not)? Does your curriculum reflect this purpose or another articulated purpose?

Further reading

Richard Bustin, *Geography Education's Potential and the Capabilities Approach: GeoCapabilities and Schools* (Cham: Palgrave Macmillan, 2019).

Alaric Maude, What might powerful geographical knowledge look like?, *Geography* 101(2) (2016): 70–76.

....

26 Maude, What might powerful geographical knowledge look like?

Part II
Practice

Chapter 6

Content

Challenging "anything is geography"

In the introduction I outlined some of the issues with the attitude that "anything is geography". This echoes a concern expressed by Alex Standish, who writes:

> When questioned about the purpose of geography, most candidates for student teaching give one of three answers: geography is "about everything", "saving the planet" or "making a difference". This means that after learning the subject at school, spending at least three years at university studying geography and deciding to enter the teaching profession, these geographers lack a conception of their discipline.[1]

This lack of disciplinary concept seems to be a greater issue in geography than in other subjects. There may be disagreements over how to teach mathematics, or why it is important, but there are fewer debates over what the school subject of mathematics *is*. Even our occasional humanities stablemate of history seems more secure in its nature.

The problem is, as discussed in Part I, the purpose that you give to a subject shapes its curriculum. If we take the geography out of the geography curriculum and replace it with "anything", "saving the planet" or "making a difference", we no longer have a geography curriculum; we have replaced it, at best, with a sub-par citizenship curriculum. To have a geography curriculum we need to take pupils on a journey through our subject with a clear destination in mind. This destination is the purpose we have just set out.

Our first step towards putting a purposeful curriculum into practice is to decide on the content of our curriculum – what is it that we want to teach our pupils about

1   Alex Standish, Geography. In Alex Standish and Alka Sehgal Cuthbert (eds), *What Should Schools Teach? Disciplines, Subjects and the Pursuit of Truth* (London: UCL Institute of Education Press, 2017), pp. 88–103 at p. 88.

geography? This is an enormous decision that falls on teachers and heads of department to make, with very little guidance on what to include at Key Stages 1–3 followed by heavy prescription at Key Stages 4 and 5. It might be tempting to see the national curriculum in England as providing the content of your own curriculum but, as the following table shows, it is remarkably light on any detail.[2] If we strip out the discussion on places to be studied (covered in the next chapter) and procedural knowledge (considered later in this chapter) we are left with this:

Key Stage 1	Key Stage 2	Key Stage 3
Identify seasonal and daily weather patterns in the United Kingdom. The location of hot and cold areas of the world in relation to the equator and the North and South Poles.	Climate zones, biomes and vegetation belts. Rivers. Mountains, volcanoes and earthquakes. The water cycle. Types of settlement and land use. Economic activity including trade links, and the distribution of natural resources including energy, food, minerals and water.	Geological timescales and plate tectonics. Rocks, weathering and soils. Weather and climate, including the change in climate from the Ice Age to the present. Glaciation, hydrology and coasts. Population and urbanisation. International development; economic activity in the primary, secondary, tertiary and quaternary sectors. Use of natural resources.

2   Table adapted from Department for Education, National curriculum in England: geography programmes of study (11 September 2013). Available at: https://www.gov.uk/government/publications/national-curriculum-in-england-geography-programmes-of-study/national-curriculum-in-england-geography-programmes-of-study.

Key Stage 1	Key Stage 2	Key Stage 3
		The interaction of human and physical processes to influence and change landscapes, environments and the climate. How human activity relies on the effective functioning of natural systems.

What these lists can lead to is an assumption that geography is taught through distinct topic blocks named things like "the water cycle" and "types of settlement". This can result in a very fragmented curriculum in which pupils move between disparate topics that seem to have little to connect them. It is worth remembering that the national curriculum does not insist that the subject is taught in this way. It could be that in Key Stage 2 a class studies the geography necessary to answer the question "How does physical geography influence different settlements?" This could include elements of all the prescribed content from the national curriculum. You might:

- Contrast settlements across South America, including looking at those of indigenous people in the Amazon Rainforest and contrasting them with those of farmers settling on the fringes.

- Consider the role that rivers play in settlement location and how settlements change rivers as well as being changed by them.

- Examine how cities cope with water stress and the impact they can have on their local water cycle.

- Study the impact of tectonic hazards on settlements and responses to them.

- Look at the ecological footprint of different settlements around the world and how they consume different resources.

One reason why it is possible to take such an approach is that the national curriculum doesn't outline any depth of coverage. It tells us to study rivers, but it doesn't tell us what to study about them. Should we study how a river changes from source to mouth? How landforms are created and change over time? The implication of rivers for people – as both a challenge and an opportunity? River management? All of this and more is possible, but it is a decision that each teacher and department need to make. To decide what to cover, what content to include, we have to return to the purpose of our curriculum. To do this we could ask, "Is this geography powerful?"

Case study: Jodie Powers

Before September 2019, our geography curriculum looked very similar to that of other schools. However, the traditional approach to covering the national curriculum in Key Stage 3 gave rise to a number of issues:

- Each year group in Key Stage 3 covered six topics. Some topics were shoehorned into a single half-term and had to be covered in as little as five weeks. Consequently, we were unable to teach topics in any significant depth.

- Individual topics were frequently planned and delivered in isolation, without links to previously taught topics.

- The curriculum was dislocated between phases. It did not stretch pupils enough, nor did it equip them with the necessary skills or foundations to be successful at Key Stage 4 or 5.

To tackle those issues, and others, we redesigned the curriculum. The first stage of that process involved identifying the core concepts which would underpin our curriculum. Taking inspiration from the A level specifications, we selected: "place", "causality", "interdependence", "risk", "adaptation", "mitigation" and "sustainability".

The second stage required consideration of our pupils' needs, and of research on types of curricula. Ultimately, we selected a spiral curriculum, revolving around a clear narrative of place.

What did the final product look like?

The curriculum is a journey across the world. Each year, pupils focus on two continents, and the geographical content relevant to them. In Year 7, we cover Europe and Asia, before moving onto Oceania and South America in Year 8, and concluding with North America and Africa in Year 9.[3] The journey begins for Year 7 pupils in the place most familiar to them, before moving to continents which are less well known. Furthermore, the difficulty level of the geographical content increases from continent to continent, and year to year.

Our previous curriculum was topic-led but, ironically, geographically confused. We now address elements of topics in the context of place, and ground each topic in the core concepts. For example, we introduce Year 7 pupils to tectonic plate movement by studying earthquakes and volcanoes in Oceania, focusing on the core concepts of causality, interdependence, risk and mitigation. In Year 8, we return to the topic when studying the formation of fold mountains in South America and tsunamis. The relevant core concepts then are causality, risk, adaptation and interdependence. Finally, in Year 9, we look at whether California could survive a catastrophic tectonic event, and at the formation and impact of the Great Rift Valley in Africa. In Year 9, all of the core concepts are addressed.

The core concepts are introduced or re-introduced at the beginning of each year. We do this by taking a geographical issue from the previous year – for example, the 2019 Amazon forest fires – and breaking it down by reference to the core concepts across two or three lessons. Interweaving content and concepts enables better recall and understanding amongst our pupils, and for them to develop a schema with much greater breadth and depth. Students' outlooks are broadened, and stereotypes and misconceptions of place are challenged. There is common geography across the world, but the causes and effects can be uncommonly different.

**Jodie Powers is head of humanities at The Bemrose School in Derby.
She tweets as @MissPowers_Geog.**

---

3   Antarctica as a continent is covered in a whole-school programme in Year 7.

Identifying powerful geography

Identifying powerful knowledge within the geography curriculum is fraught with difficulty. As Alaric Maude has explained, and as discussed in Chapter 2, there are two different ways of defining powerful knowledge in the curriculum, based on:[4]

1   The characteristics of the knowledge; especially in relation to how it was created.

2   What the knowledge enables those who hold it to do.

What Maude's work in unpicking these definitions does is help to give us criteria that we can use to evaluate the power of our own curriculum decisions.

Firstly, he explains the limitations of using the definition of powerful knowledge in terms of its characteristic as something created in academic disciplines. School geography is not the same as academic geography, as teachers must seek to recontextualise the academic field into something appropriate for younger pupils who do not yet have the foundational knowledge to fully access it. The field of geography is also incredibly broad and contains any number of sub-disciplines – such as urban geography or development studies – and almost anything you wanted to teach could be linked to *something* being discussed somewhere in a university geography department. Unfortunately, this does not get us beyond the "anything is geography" difficulty.

What is important, though, is that we as recontextualisers of academic geography do have an awareness of what academic geography looks like and that this awareness is as up to date as it can be. Our powerful curriculum needs its links to the discipline. We can maintain these links through engagement with subject associations and their journals, in particular the Geographical Association's *Geography*, as well as continuing to read widely around our subject from recently published books. Many universities continue to offer lectures to teachers, and online webinars that are free to attend, as well as massive open online courses (MOOCs), also often free.

I would suggest that it is in Maude's second definition of powerful knowledge, based on what it enables the learner to do, that we find the most useful guide to the content we might want for our purposeful curriculum. He highlights how

---

4   Maude, What might powerful geographical knowledge look like?

Michael Young points to the following six things that people will be enabled to do through their powerful knowledge:

1   Discover new ways of thinking.

2   Better explain and understand the natural and social worlds.

3   Think about alternative futures and what they could do to influence them.

4   Have some power over their own knowledge.

5   Be able to engage in current debates of significance.

6   Go beyond the limits of their personal experience.

Maude then transforms this into five types of powerful geographical knowledge, and I would suggest that we could apply this as a set of criteria to evaluate the curriculum we offer our pupils.

1. Does it provide new ways of thinking?

Geography is a subject rich in big ideas that allow us to think about the world in new ways, as we saw, for example, in Peter Jackson's list of the grammar underlying our subject (see page 58). These big ideas do not form the content of the curriculum but rather sit behind it; they are ways of approaching the content. For example, if we were to teach pupils about the coast, we might consider it through the lens of each of these big ideas. We could view the coast as a place that is viewed and experienced differently by different groups of people. Some of them might see it as a hazard to be managed, whereas for others it is a facility to be enjoyed. We could also view it as a space shaped by physical processes and seek to understand why the same processes operate differently on different stretches of coastline. We can also look at coasts through the lens of the environment and the interaction between physical and human environments. We might study how people have affected physical processes, such as through the building of groynes, but also how changes in the physical environment are leading to adaptations in the human environment, such as from the threat of rising sea levels and increased storm activity.

As such, when we are teaching about coastal landforms and management, we are not *only* teaching the propositional knowledge (as important as this is) but also the way in which geographers view this knowledge and put it together to think in deeper ways about our world.

2. Does it help our pupils to explain and understand the world?

The term "geography" refers to "writing the world". Our curriculum should give pupils the ability to understand why the world is the way it is and explain their thoughts to others. This might mean them grappling with geographical data so that they can understand spatial distribution. For example, we might use geographic information systems (GIS) to allow them to see how neighbourhood-level data on affluence aligns with data on air pollution, to help them explain health inequalities. We might also introduce them to statistical techniques to help them explore the strength of correlation, starting with simple scatter graphs and lines of best fit and continuing over the years to include tests of statistical significance, and to help them understand that many factors operate in real-world scenarios.

Other processes might result from simpler causation that helps to explain why the world is the way it is, such as the processes that result in the movement of sediment along the coast. When pupils understand this, the explanation can bring order to what can appear to be chaos. Again, though, the aim here isn't *only* for them to understand how longshore drift operates but to develop the ability to explain its implications, such as the way in which a beach may be starved of sediment due to the building of groynes elsewhere in the sediment cell.

By analysing information and understanding causal relationships, we are helping pupils to form generalisations. In order to form an accurate generalisation, we need to know enough about the world to see common features and common explanations. For example, a geographer might generalise that "the imposition of hard engineering on the coast often has unintended consequences for communities down drift". Maude points out that the power of generalisation lies in going further than simply explaining what *is*, arguing that:

> **Generalisations can be especially powerful if they contain explanatory mechanisms and, therefore, they can be used to predict.**[5]

5   Maude, What might powerful geographical knowledge look like?, 73.

In this example, the pupil would now be able to make predictions about the consequences of building a terminal groyne on other communities. Their view of the world has been transformed by powerful knowledge to the point where they can see into the future.

3. Does it give them power over what they know?

To have power over what we know we need to have an understanding of where the knowledge came from and how it was reached. This is one of the key differences between Future 1 and Future 3 views of knowledge and the curriculum. We want to ensure that our curriculum gives pupils the opportunity to explore where the information we use has come from and the ability to critique this knowledge and the way in which it is presented.

Both the geography GCSE and A level specifications highlight this aspect of geographical knowledge, with the expectation that pupils will have a good understanding of reliability and validity, as well as the ability to suggest the most appropriate way of displaying data and an understanding of the misinterpretations that might result from poorly displayed data. This way of critically appraising the creation and presentation of knowledge can be built in throughout the key stages through an enquiry approach (see Chapter 9).

Another way to gain power over what we know is to be able to find and make sense of information for ourselves. Learning journeys should not end when we leave an educational setting. We want our pupils to become enquiring adults – ones who can continue to explore the world geographically.

4. Does it mean that young people can join in conversations and debates?

Education gives us a common language, which gives us the ability to participate in society at different levels. It should mean that a pupil will, in the future, be able to join in a discussion about the best way of approaching coastal management in their town or about the UK's obligation, or not, to get involved in a conflict on the other side of the world. They should hold an informed view on climate change, justify the decisions they make and be aware that their choices in life can have a far-reaching and nuanced impact on the world around them.

Our ability to join in with these conversations is not based on generic critical thinking skills but rather on the knowledge that we possess on these topics: knowledge that is highly geographical in nature. Pupils will need a broad geography curriculum to prepare them for such conversations – one that reveals the complex interactions between the topics we teach so that they can draw on ideas from across the domain in making an argument or reaching a conclusion. For example, in order to understand a conflict brewing in the Middle East, they may need to understand aspects of development studies, resource management, colonialism, economic geography and geopolitics. The geography curriculum will hopefully have shown them how to put these different aspects of the subject together.

5. Does it give them knowledge of the world?

You'd hope that this last enabler would be a given in the geography classroom, but – as has been discussed throughout this book – powerful knowledge should take pupils beyond their existing, everyday experiences and expose them to ideas and places that they would not otherwise encounter. We can ask of our curriculum, what will our pupils leave the classroom knowing that they would not have known without this lesson? We might want to start a topic on coasts by looking at the local area and the features of which they are aware, but we'd want them to leave the classroom seeing them in a new way and then come back the following lesson to see how the same processes shape the coast differently elsewhere.

Non-powerful content

In some ways, identifying powerful content is the easy part of the process. Far harder can be realising what is not powerful content and then removing this from our curriculum. We can find ourselves using criteria like this to justify the inclusion of almost anything, and so we return to "anything is geography". It might be easier to see what makes content powerful by looking at an example of how it can be largely absent.

I remember a Year 8 lesson I taught on the geography of crime that was graded outstanding. It was based in part on materials from a Key Stage 3 textbook – although obviously I couldn't use the textbook in the lesson as I was being observed and using textbooks was frowned upon for not being innovative enough. The lesson looked at the idea of different types of crime and began with a classification activity (classification being seen as a desirable transferable skill). Pupils sorted cards showing different types of crime into categories. There was no right or wrong answer and they could decide what categories they should use. It was about them discussing it in groups (group discussion being seen as very important – it was hoped that it would develop those group work skills that employers want).

They then read an account of a crime that had taken place: two perpetrators had been charged and sentenced to prison for a mugging. They had to discuss the case in groups and conclude whether this was a good decision (decision making being seen as yet another important transferable skill), justifying that decision based on the evidence (there were about three short paragraphs of "evidence" to base this decision on) and the views of stakeholders (another of those very important skills – seeing the world from the perspective of others).

There was then a task which had the pupils looking at a map showing where different types of crime had been committed. They had to work out why the crimes took place in these locations, explaining why they thought this (explaining why you think things – another skill).

For the plenary they answered some multiple-choice questions by moving to different parts of the room to show what they thought (moving around, we were told, would help the kinaesthetic learners). The questions asked about their opinions. Pupils would justify their opinion and then their peers could move if they were convinced.

This lesson was entirely typical for the time and is still something I see in my role as a specialist leader of education (SLE) as I go into different schools around the country. So, what is the problem? Let us look at it in terms of what the pupils have been enabled to do.

1. Does it provide new ways of thinking?

The big ideas of geography were largely absent from this lesson. The location of the crime was kept fairly generic and could have been anywhere. There was a little bit of work done on the idea that crime might change people's attitudes towards a place, but this was only reached if pupils stumbled upon it. They weren't pointed to this as an idea that geographers might be interested in exploring.

2. Does it help our pupils to explain and understand the world?

There is not a great deal of information here for pupils to use to analyse patterns, explain trends or form generalisations. The map task had the potential to do this, but the focus was not on identifying actual trends in crime – for which they would have needed more information – but on the skill of explaining an opinion. The geographical facts fade into the background here.

3. Does it give them power over what they know?

For a lesson that is purportedly about skills development, there is a real lack of *geographical* skills being developed through disciplinary thinking. Information is given about the views of different people, but there is nothing on whether these people are representative of the wider community; there is a cartographic representation of crime data, but no time given to consider its limitations in reaching wider conclusions.

4. Does it mean that young people can join in conversations and debates?

This might be where we would hope that such a lesson would come into its own with the time spent on group discussion about the problems with crime – a conversation that, sadly, is likely to occur throughout our pupils' lives. However, although they are encouraged to talk about crime, it is from a position of ignorance. At no point are they taught about the factors that influence crime rates; instead they are meant to glean them from one map of crime statistics. Nor are they taught about the implications of different penal systems; they are simply expected to form their own opinion. Although ignorance may not stop people entering a conversation, I am not sure that this is something schools should be encouraging.

5. Does it give them knowledge of the world?

Looking back on this lesson now – and on the various iterations of it which I have seen taught over the years – I couldn't tell you what the pupils would walk out of the classroom knowing, understanding or being able to do that they didn't know, or couldn't do, coming in. There is a real lack of geography in this lesson. Instead we have a lesson on what can probably best be described as citizenship, but watered down by a desire to teach transferable skills rather than teach pupils about the world.

Although I am critical of the way in which generic skills took centre stage in this lesson, this is not to downplay the importance of geographical skills as content in the curriculum.

Procedural content in the curriculum

As discussed in Chapter 2, the debate around the relative importance of skills and knowledge in our subject has been a long one, and is also something of a false dichotomy. Skills are what we develop through the practice of procedural knowledge; procedural knowledge, the ways in which geography is *done*, is of vital importance to a powerful geography curriculum.

As with other forms of knowledge, we can see procedural knowledge spelt out in the national curriculum for Key Stages 1–3, as shown in the table that follows.[6] The GCSE and A level specifications will be discussed at the end of this chapter.

6   Table adapted from Department for Education, National curriculum in England: geography programmes of study.

Key Stage 1	Key Stage 2	Key Stage 3
Use world maps, atlases and globes. Use simple compass directions and locational and directional language to describe the location of features and routes on a map. Use aerial photographs and plan perspectives to recognise landmarks and basic human and physical features; devise a simple map; and use and construct basic symbols in a key. Use simple fieldwork and observational skills to study the geography of their school and its grounds and the key human and physical features of its surrounding environment.	Use maps, atlases, globes and digital/computer mapping to locate countries and describe features. Use the eight points of a compass, 4- and 6-figure grid references, symbols and key (including the use of Ordnance Survey maps). Use fieldwork to observe, measure, record and present the human and physical features in the local area using a range of methods, including sketch maps, plans and graphs, and digital technologies.	Build on their knowledge of globes, maps and atlases, and apply and develop this knowledge routinely in the classroom and in the field. Interpret Ordnance Survey maps in the classroom and in the field, including using grid references and scale, topographical and other thematic mapping, and aerial and satellite photographs. Use GIS to view, analyse and interpret places and data. Use fieldwork in contrasting locations to collect, analyse and draw conclusions from geographical data, using multiple sources of increasingly complex information.

We can see here that there are a few broad areas running across the skills and fieldwork section of the national curriculum:

- Using maps.
- Describing location and features.

- Recording and analysing data from fieldwork.

- Using GIS (at Key Stage 3).

What is notable by its absence is any suggestion that geographers might need to analyse different forms of information, quantitative and qualitative, at times outside of completing fieldwork. There is also no mention of the ability to write geographically, such as developing the skill of substantiating a conclusion with reference to data, or of the ability to evaluate geographical data. All of these elements need to be included in the content of a powerful geography curriculum as, to go back to Maude's criteria, they enable pupils to have power over what they know and to join in conversations and debates.[7]

An expanded list of procedural knowledge might therefore look like this (the italics are my suggested additions):

- Using maps.

- *Interpreting cartographic displays of information.*

- Describing location and features.

- *Describing spatial distribution.*

- Recording and analysing data from fieldwork.

- *Analysing data from secondary sources.*

- *Presenting data (in the form of graphical, cartographic and diagrammatic displays).*

- Using GIS (at Key Stage 3).

- *Reaching and substantiating conclusions.*

- *Evaluating the reliability and validity of data.*

Each of these can, of course, be expanded. For example, using maps:

> Using 4- and 6-figure grid references.

> Identifying relief using contour lines.

> Using maps to support decision making.

7   Maude, What might powerful geographical knowledge look like?

The task of drawing out all the geography-specific skills that we want our pupils to develop can be a useful activity for a department or year group team meeting and will, as with everything, come down to how you see the purpose of your curriculum. We are teaching the procedural knowledge, and allowing time to develop the skills necessary for this purpose to be put into practice. Once these decisions have been taken, we need to ensure that our chosen content is placed into the curriculum in a logical sequence, with regular opportunities for it to be revisited and built upon (see Chapter 8).

Threshold, core and hinterland content

Another consideration when selecting curricular content is organising it according to threshold concepts, core knowledge and what could be considered hinterland content. The idea of threshold concepts was developed by economics lecturers Jan Meyer and Ray Land, who noticed that their pupils seemed to be blocked by the same recurring barriers. They identified certain ideas that were so fundamental to their subject that pupils were unable to make progress if not secure in their understanding of them.[8] They termed these ideas "threshold concepts" and suggested that they are:[9]

- Transformative: they change the way in which you see the world.

- Troublesome: they might seem counterintuitive or alien.

- Irreversible: the transformative nature means that once they are learnt, the concepts are unlikely to be forgotten.

- Integrated: they reveal connections between the different parts of the discipline.

- Bounded: despite this, these concepts only apply within defined parameters.

- Discursive: they lead to the development of new language.

---

8 Jan H. F. Meyer and Ray Land, Threshold concepts and troublesome knowledge: linkages to ways of thinking and practising within the disciplines. In Chris Rust (ed.), *Improving Student Learning: Theory and Practice Ten Years On* (Oxford: Oxford Centre for Staff and Learning Development, 2003), pp. 412–424.
9 Mark Enser, *Making Every Geography Lesson Count: Six Principles to Support Great Geography Teaching* (Carmarthen: Crown House Publishing, 2018).

Even with this list to help us, it can be difficult to pin down exactly what would count as a threshold concept. In some ways, this is a good thing as the debate over what counts is a useful one to have as a department – different colleagues will make their case for different ideas to be included. You could argue that "sustainability" is a threshold concept: if pupils have not understood it, and have mistaken it for general environmental concerns, they are likely to be confused in many subsequent lessons featuring economic and social considerations. Others might make a similar case for an understanding of longshore drift and the impact it has on pupils' understanding of other coastal processes and the landforms they create.

A similar powerful discussion can be had over which knowledge is considered *core* and which is considered *hinterland*. Core knowledge is that which you want pupils to walk away with and be able to retrieve and use in the future: the kind of knowledge that you feel an educated person should have. This could be anything from the way in which rivers carve out waterfalls to the problems with using gross national product (GNP) as a measure of development. Hinterland knowledge is that which pupils need to have access to in the lesson to support them in gaining core knowledge, but which we know they might not have to hand in years to come. We might teach them about the weaknesses of GNP by telling them about the example of Nigeria, whose GNP jumped after they started including the emergent media and technology industries in the figures. This story – the hinterland knowledge – might not be recalled in the future, but it supported the learning of the core information. We can ensure that pupils focus on the core information by being explicit about what this is. This could be by ensuring that any activities are based on the use of the core information, returning to the core information at the end of the lesson and in subsequent lessons, its inclusion in knowledge organisers, retrieval quizzes and ongoing assessments. For this to work, it is vital that we as teachers are clear which knowledge is core and which is hinterland so that we teach them appropriately.

Content at Key Stages 4 and 5

This chapter has focused on the discussions we need to have when deciding on the content to include in our curriculum and has largely considered this for Key Stages 1–3. This is because the suggested content for these key stages is remarkably light (see the table on page 82), whereas there is a great deal of prescription at GCSE and A level, with exam specifications detailing this content running to several pages. However, there are still decisions to be made, especially over the places to be studied (discussed in Chapter 7) and also the supporting hinterland content.

For example, an exam specification might insist that pupils are taught about different types of aid schemes, and even list the types (multilateral, bilateral, emergency, long-term, etc.), but which examples will you use to support the learning? Most exam specifications will need typifying through examples, and choosing these is an important curriculum decision.

Case study: Denise Freeman

I have always encouraged my students to ask critical questions about the information they are presented with in the classroom, but in recent years I have looked for ways to make this more explicit. My interest in doing this has been supported by a growing focus on powerful knowledge in schools, and, in particular, subject-specialist knowledge. In the case of geography, specialist knowledge is usually developed by academics or researchers working in a university setting. I have therefore looked for ways to make links between academic geography and school geography, and to help pupils explore the roots of the discipline. I want my pupils to consider where geographical knowledge comes from: from which perspective? Why does someone have this view? Why are we studying it? Is there a counterview? By exploring such questions, they can begin to understand where school geography comes from and make connections between the knowledge they study in school and the work that academics do.

To help my post-16 pupils make connections with academic geography, I began introducing them to some of the most influential traditions within the discipline. To do this I created a simple written guide to perspectives such as positivism, radical approaches, humanistic geography and postmodernism. I referred to some undergraduate texts to help me (after contacting a local university to ask for a reading list). Morgan and Lambert also provide a really useful historical account of the development of geography, which helped me produce the document for the pupils.[10] I wanted my class to understand that geographical knowledge isn't just created by teachers, textbooks or exam boards; it comes from a wider discipline – a discipline that is shaped through research, discussion and debate. Discussing a range of academic perspectives introduces pupils to the idea that there are many different ways of thinking about the world – different ways of thinking geographically. Furthermore, there are multiple geographies to be studied and explored: cultural, social, economic, political, feminist and environmental geographies to name a few.

My A level group was then asked to go away and produce an icon or image to sum up each of the key traditions within academic geography. This activity produced some really interesting results, which showed a good understanding of the new knowledge they had been exposed to. I then attempted to place this new knowledge into context: to apply it to school geography. I did this through the changing places unit on the A level curriculum. This unit appears to have been shaped by many aspects of the humanistic and cultural perspectives within geography, but with links to social science and structuralist perspectives. The curriculum asks pupils to consider how different people (and groups of people) feel about the place in which they live, and the relationship they may have with their surroundings, as well as exploring issues of power, governance and inequality. Using my guide to academic geography, the pupils were able to make connections between what they were studying and the powerful disciplinary knowledge presented by academics.

As well as trying to explore some of the roots of geographical knowledge, the class were exposed, at particular points during the topic, to extracts from academic texts or research. At times this connected directly with what they were

---

10 John Morgan and David Lambert, *Geography: Teaching School Subjects 11–19* (Abingdon and New York: Routledge, 2005).

studying – for example, research on gentrification – at other times the text took them beyond the confines of the school curriculum. For example, the group had shown an interest in the relationship between ethnicity and rural tourism. I used some academic writing by Paul Cloke to encourage them to think geographically about this issue. In another example, I used academic texts about youth geographies to consider how different people feel about places. These texts exposed the group to powerful disciplinary knowledge, written by specialists in their field. Moving forward I intend to make further links with academic geography as we study other topics on the syllabus, particularly those connected more with physical geography and the environmental sciences. I am also keen to make use of *Routes*, the journal for pupil geographers, and to encourage my pupils to consider submitting some of their own writing to the publication.

Denise Freeman is a geography teacher at Oaks Park High School in London. She tweets as @geography_DAF.

Questions

- Pick one topic from your current curriculum – to what extent does it develop the five types of powerful knowledge outlined by Maude?

- For this same topic – what knowledge is core and what is hinterland?

- For this same topic – what are the threshold concepts that pupils *must* understand in order to make progress?

Further reading

Nicholas Clifford and Alex Standish, Physical geography. In Mark Jones (ed.), *Handbook of Secondary Geography* (Sheffield: The Geographical Association, 2017), pp. 62–75.

Peter Jackson, Human geography. In Mark Jones (ed.), *Handbook of Secondary Geography* (Sheffield: The Geographical Association, 2017), pp. 76–91.

Chapter 7

Places

As with many of the decisions made about how to fill a geography curriculum, the choices of places to study can often seem a little arbitrary. Indeed, often the places studied aren't the choice of the current teacher but were the remnants of decisions made by previous teams whose rationale may now be lost in the mists of time but whose schemes of work continue to be taught. I was recently in a school in which the geography department were still using South Korea as an example of a newly emerging economy simply because it is what their programme of study listed. The data they were using stemmed from the 1980s.

At other times a place may be chosen because there are resources available in the textbook, the school or local community has a link to it, the teacher knows something about it, or it is currently featured in the news. Each of these criteria has something to recommend it, but what is often missing is a curricular justification for the inclusion of the place. How does the study of this place help us to realise the stated purpose of our curriculum?

This chapter considers the role that the study of place plays in putting the purpose of our curriculum into practice, as well as the role that the study of regions can play in helping pupils develop powerful knowledge about the world. Our aim here is to study place in such a way that it affords opportunities to think geographically by revealing the many layers that give a sense of place.

Developing an understanding of "place"

Ever since geography was established as an academic discipline at the end of the 19th and beginning of the 20th century there have been debates and discussions about what is meant by a study of place. However, the fact that place, by any definition, is central to the study of geography has never really been in question. From Mackinder's argument in 1887 that "geography is the study of distribution"[1] to Tim Cresswell, in 2015, saying:

> Place is one of the two or three most important terms for my discipline – geography. If pushed, I would argue that it is the most important of them all.[2]

We can see that geography is viewed very much in terms of not just processes but the location in which the processes occur.

Between the time of Mackinder's writing and Cresswell's there has been a seismic shift in how place is approached in geography, at least in geography as an academic discipline. Historically, geography – from ancient Greek and Roman thinkers through to the early 20th century – largely saw the study of place as being descriptive. The purpose of geographical study was to represent different places as accurately as possible using increasingly positivistic, quantifiable methods.[3] Geographers such as Alexander Humboldt working in the Americas sought to explain the unique characteristics of different regions by exploring the different geographical layers that make them up (climate, ecosystems, hydrology, geology, etc.). The aim, in part, was to explain how these spatial distributions led to the development of unique cultural, or human, geography.

After the Second World War there was a move away from this descriptive approach to place towards what Eleanor Rawling refers to as a social-constructionist approach: what in Michael Young's terminology is thought of as Future 2. This approach built on the work of critical geographies, such as Marxist, feminist, post-colonial and post-structuralist geographies. In this approach there was a

---

1   Halford Mackinder, On the scope and methods of geography, *Proceedings of the Royal Geographical Society and Monthly Record of Geography* 9(3) (1887): 141–174 at 160.
2   Tim Cresswell, *Place: An Introduction*, 2nd edn (Chichester: Wiley Blackwell, 2015), p. 1.
3   Eleanor Rawling, Place in geography: change and challenge. In Mark Jones and David Lambert (eds), *Debates in Geography Education*, 2nd edn (Abingdon and New York: Routledge, 2018), pp. 49–61.

greater effort to understand how places were shaped by cultural, political and economic conditions, and to explore a greater variety of voices. As with other approaches to knowledge in Future 2, there was a belief that ideas about place were socially constructed and that there could be no one true representation of a place; instead, we needed to look at the area through different critical lenses. There was also a move away from seeing places as being bounded, looking at them, instead, in a more global context to better understand how different, complex connections were shaping them.

This social-constructionist approach has been developed further into a phenomenological approach which considers the role that places play in shaping us as humans. In this approach to the subject, ethnogeographies – individual accounts of people's lived experience – are common.[4] Here geographers concern themselves particularly with the idea of how people experience places and how place is being-in-the-world. This moves us a long way from the positivist approaches of Humboldt and his attempts to define and fix the exact nature of places.

Denise Freeman and Alun Morgan agree with Rawling's assertion that school geography should include a study of place using all three of these approaches (positivist, social constructivist and phenomenological – although they define these as positivist, social scientific and humanistic, but they overlap to a significant degree).[5] Using all three approaches in our curriculum, they argue, should help our pupils to develop a better disciplinary knowledge though understanding different ways in which geographers think about a central component of the subject. However, Liz Taylor argues that in actual fact there is little real exploration of the meaning of place in school geography.[6] Have we really moved past the positivistic/descriptive idea of place? If not, a solution might be to widen our understanding and application of regional geography in our curriculum.

4   Fran Martin, Ethnogeography: towards liberatory geography education, *Children's Geographies* 6(4) (2008): 437–450.
5   Denise Freeman and Alun Morgan, Place and locational knowledge. In Mark Jones (ed.), *Handbook of Secondary Geography* (Sheffield: The Geographical Association, 2017), pp. 120–133
6   Liz Taylor, Place: an exploration, *Teaching Geography* 30(1) (2005): 14–17.

What is "regional geography" and why does it matter?

Regional geography has often been associated with an old-fashioned approach, sometimes characterised as the "capes and bays" approach, in which pupils are expected to memorise the salient characteristics of different parts of the world. We can even see this parodied in Sue Townsend's popular Adrian Mole series, in Adrian's pride in his knowledge of the Norwegian leather industry following an in-depth project in his geography lessons. However, as Alex Standish explains:

> regional geography is intimately related to systematic (or thematic) geography and the failure to maintain the relationship between the two ultimately undermines the credibility of both.[7]

This regional approach to the curriculum involves studying a part of the world in detail to note the factors that interact in order to shape it. This needs to go much further than case studies of places to typify particular themes or issues (Mumbai for the impacts of urbanisation, Boscastle for the floods, the Amazon for deforestation, and so on) and instead concentrate on the place in light of all the geography operating there. We are moving beyond a purely thematic approach to the discipline.

Standish points to the work of Kant, in his years as a lecturer in geography, in dividing the subject into two: thematic and regional geography. Thematic geography involves studying the processes that affect the earth's surface in turn, often giving us our topics in the school geography curriculum: tectonics, oceans, rivers, migration, urbanisation, etc. This approach has a hierarchical structure, with a search for ever greater precision, certainty and truth. Each theme, or topic, can be studied in depth to develop models of behaviour, such as the demographic transition model (population), Bradshaw model (rivers) or central tendency model (urbanisation). These "truths" give us propositional knowledge, and learning about how these "truths" were reached and are contested helps with procedural knowledge. What is missing is contextual knowledge.

---

7   Alex Standish, The place of regional geography. In Mark Jones and David Lambert (eds), *Debates in Geography Education*, 2nd edn (Abingdon and New York: Routledge, 2018) pp. 62–74 at p. 66.

This contextual knowledge can be developed through a regional approach. Here, the models and theories developed by thematic geography can be studied and tested in real places. As we study different places, we use a horizontal structure that builds out sideward; we accumulate knowledge at a similar level of depth, but about more places, and so widen our view of the world. This regional approach also allows us to look for connections between themes that would otherwise be lost. For example, if we were studying a region such as South Asia, we may see how the economic geography of tourism affects the ecosystem through deforestation, which then changes the catchment hydrology, which causes flooding. This may also help us to see the need for global governance of catchments that cross national boundaries (political geography) and ways to deal with the aftermath of the floods as land is lost, causing people to migrate into the cities. A study limited to the individual themes would miss those connections and it is finding the connections that turns a disparate field into *geography* as a unified discipline.

How do we select places to study?

To put all of this into practice, we first need to select places to study. To an extent, for teachers in England at least, the national curriculum does some of the selection for us; although, as discussed in Chapter 2, there is still a lot of agency left to the individual teacher or department. The national curriculum separates out place knowledge from locational knowledge, even though many aspects listed under locational knowledge contain the kind of descriptive knowledge familiar to the regional/descriptive approach to the subject common in England until the second half of the 20th century. The table that follows shows the locational knowledge outlined in the national curriculum:[8]

Key Stage	Locational knowledge
Key Stage 1	The world's seven continents and five oceans. Characteristics of the four countries of the United Kingdom and its surrounding seas.

8   Department for Education, National curriculum in England: geography programmes of study.

Key Stage	Locational knowledge
Key Stage 2	The world's countries, using maps to focus on Europe (including the location of Russia) and North and South America, concentrating on their environmental regions, key physical and human characteristics, countries, and major cities. The United Kingdom, geographical regions and their identifying human and physical characteristics, key topographical features (including hills, mountains, coasts and rivers), and land-use patterns; and understand how some of these aspects have changed over time.
Key Stage 3	Extend their locational knowledge and deepen their spatial awareness of the world's countries, using maps of the world to focus on Africa, Russia, Asia (including China and India), and the Middle East, focusing on their environmental regions, including polar and hot deserts, key physical and human characteristics, countries and major cities.

Whereas in the next table we can see how place knowledge has been specified:[9]

Key Stage	Places to be studied mentioned
Key Stage 1	Understand geographical similarities and differences through studying the human and physical geography of a small area of the United Kingdom, and of a small area in a contrasting non-European country.
Key Stage 2	Understand geographical similarities and differences through the study of human and physical geography of a region of the United Kingdom, a region in a European country, and a region in North or South America.

---

9   Department for Education, National curriculum in England: geography programmes of study.

Key Stage	Places to be studied mentioned
Key Stage 3	Understand geographical similarities, differences and links between places through the study of the human and physical geography of a region in Africa and a region in Asia.

As we can see, there is a lot more detail given for the locational knowledge that needs to be included than for the place knowledge. We can also see that, generally, there is a move away from the UK over the key stages: from a focus there at Key Stage 1, to a focus on Europe and the Americas in Key Stage 2, to a complete absence in Key Stage 3, with a widening global focus taking in Asia and Africa. Australasia and Antarctica remain absent throughout. There is also a move away from places being studied in a "small area", such as the location around the school or the local community, to wider, and potentially more distant, regions, such as a region within Africa. What is lacking is an opportunity to revisit places studied in previous years, with a possible exception of returning to the small area of a non-European country studied in Key Stage 1 as a contrast to one in the UK. To a great extent this is due to practical constraints. Most secondary schools will have pupils from dozens of feeder primary schools, all of whom will have studied different places. It is, however, a weakness in the model that we should be aware of when planning our curriculum for any key stage; this may be the only time our pupils will encounter this place in their school studies.

Although the national curriculum gives us a starting point in selecting places to study, it is only the vaguest of starting points. At Key Stage 1 pupils will study any small area of the UK and contrast it to any small area of any non-European country. That gives an almost limitless number of options. The same is broadly true of each key stage, especially given the lose definition of the word "region". So how do we select places to study?

Firstly, we want to consider an important argument made by Mary Biddulph: we need to be aware of the danger of presenting a single story when we talk about places in geography.[10] This often happens when places are seen only as case studies to typify particular points that we want to make. For example:

- Nepal becomes nothing more than a low-income country that struggled to deal with the impacts of an earthquake.

10 Mary Biddulph, Editorial: "the danger of a single story", *Teaching Geography* 36(2) (2011): 45.

- India is a place where rapid urbanisation has created huge slums in the city that the authorities cannot deal with.

- Boscastle is a place where there was a severe flood that resulted in a number of new engineering approaches being adopted.

- Brazil is the home of the Amazon Rainforest, which is being deforested to make way for farmland.

Complex places are thus reduced to little more than a headline. This can be a particular issue at GCSE, as case studies and examples are often required by the exam board to showcase very particular ideas. Pupils *need* to have an example of an earthquake or volcanic eruption in a low-income country largely to prove the point that they struggle more to manage the risk. At this stage there is little requirement for them to really understand the complexities of the place in terms of the other geographies affecting it. Yet if we want to create a powerful curriculum, that is exactly what we need them to do.

Secondly, we can consider the purpose of our curriculum in developing our pupils' powerful knowledge. We want to select places that will have the greatest power in helping them make sense of the world and moving them beyond their everyday experiences. Making these kinds of decisions as teachers, however, requires us to have a very deep knowledge of the wider world and its regions. Without this, we are likely to fall back on the single stories we were warned about by Biddulph. For example, we could decide to study North Africa as a region with the purpose of helping pupils to understand patterns of migration into southern Europe. However, many of the migrants passing through this region originated in other areas, in West and East Africa, and so an understanding of the drivers for migration actually involve a study of these regions, not of North Africa itself. We also run the risk, by studying North Africa, of retelling a story that our pupils will encounter about this part of the world on their own: crisis hit, drought prone and beset by conflict. It will probably be more powerful to tell a different story.

This also creates a tension between selecting places because they are often in the news, and therefore more likely to help our pupils make sense of what they are encountering, or including places that are highly significant to world events but whose stories may not be told as often. For example, it is common for Key Stage 3 curricula to look at China as the chosen region in Asia. This is not surprising as this country is a rising superpower whose influence is felt all over the world. It makes an interesting regional study in terms of population (the impacts of anti-natal policies), urbanisation (the growth of ghost cities) and its global influence (industrialisation, foreign investment, conflict over ocean territories, etc.). There is a compelling argument in favour of studying this region.

However, China is a country that our pupils will encounter – in the news, in conversation, in documentaries, and so on – with or without us. Perhaps it would be more powerful to study regions in Asia that are often ignored completely (the Central Asian 'stans', for example) or only covered from one angle (such as the Middle East). In an ideal world pupils would, of course, study both, but with limited time these kinds of trade-offs are inevitable.

Thirdly, we want to consider how we can create opportunities to revisit places to help build up a more complex picture of the regions studied. As already mentioned, there is a system-wide issue with doing this across the Key Stage 2–3 break, but primary schools could look to build a cohesive curriculum from Key Stage 1 to 2, and secondary schools from Key Stage 3 to 4, and even into Key Stage 5. This affords some opportunities to build on prior knowledge. For example, in Key Stage 1 pupils might look at a small area of a non-European country with the purpose of simply identifying how different it is from their own small area of the UK. This non-European country could be in North or South America, so they can come back to look at it in more detail at Key Stage 2 (when the national curriculum specifies that they look at an example from the Americas).

Likewise, it should be possible to forward-plan for Key Stage 4 when selecting places to study at Key Stage 3. Previously, I gave the example of Nepal being used as a case study to tell the single story of its response to an earthquake. This would be less of an issue if, in Key Stage 3, pupils had already looked at the region of the Indian subcontinent and developed a greater understanding of its people, culture, politics and environments. They would then be able to place the response to the earthquake in a wider context due to their deeper knowledge of the area.

As ever in geography, the curriculum decisions we make are never simple. We have an entire world to introduce our pupils to, and usually very limited time in which to do it. Consequently, the final part of this chapter will consider what it might look like to put this decision making into practice.

Putting it into practice: place in the curriculum

Both approaches to the curriculum – thematic and regional – have their drawbacks:

- A thematic approach may lead to a fragmented study of the subject, meaning that greater geographical conclusions that require an understanding of a combination of themes are never reached.

- A regional approach may mean that pupils do not gain the depth of knowledge they require in order to really understand the processes that shape our planet across different regions. They may develop good knowledge of the chosen case studies but miss the opportunity to apply it to other areas of the world.

It therefore seems clear that we need to create a curriculum that includes both thematic and regional approaches. Chapter 8 will consider how we might go about sequencing the curriculum to allow for this dual approach, but let us first consider how we could select the places to include.

We could begin by considering a place against the following criteria:

- Does this place take pupils beyond their everyday experiences?

- Will studying this place lead to the development of powerful geographical knowledge?

- Do I, as a teacher, know enough about this place to teach it powerfully?

- Can I find the information I need to teach this place effectively?

- Does this place help to build on knowledge of places and locations studied previously?

- Does this place allow us to tell a complex story and avoid simple headlines?

For example, at Key Stage 2 we might have the initial idea to study the south of Spain as a region of a European country, focusing on climate and the tourism industry. In its favour is that we are likely to have enough knowledge of this region to teach it, and we would be able to find information to help us teach it easily. However, the fact that the south of Spain is hot and attracts tourists is not going to move many pupils beyond the everyday knowledge that they could gain without these lessons. It may also risk overlooking the complexity of the place and falling into a "sun, sand and siestas" simple summary.

This is not to say that Spain should not be used as a regional study; we just need to shift the focus slightly and consider which geographical lenses to apply. If we are going to study climate and tourism, then it would be interesting to consider the impacts that tourism has on a place with low average annual precipitation and the water shortages that result. This would be an interesting starting point, but it still falls into the trap of the simple story that tourism is "bad". More interesting still would be to contrast the impacts of tourism with those of farming in the region – which generates greater benefits for the amount of water used? Here we have moved from the simple story of "sun, sand and siestas" to the still simple "here is a problem with tourism" to the more complex geographical enquiry question "Is farming or tourism more sustainable in a water-stressed area?" (For more on enquiry in geography see Chapter 9.)

Once we have selected places to study, we need to consider what prior knowledge we want to draw on to help pupils understand the complexity of these places: the thematic geography they will apply. For example, at Key Stage 3 we are directed by the national curriculum to consider a region in Africa – the physical and human characteristics and the links between places. There are any number of potentially exciting regional studies that could be done here, focusing on a range of questions:

● Why are migrants passing through North Africa?

● Why is conflict brewing in the Horn of Africa?

● How is East Africa overcoming barriers to development?

● What has been the legacy of colonialism in West Africa?

● How is foreign investment shaping southern Africa?

For our regional study to be successful a large amount of prior knowledge will need to be brought to bear. Let us take the East Africa question as an example.

Pupils could use:

● Their knowledge of tectonic processes to explain how this has shaped the region and affected the people who live there.

- What they know about development indicators to test the idea that barriers to development are being overcome.

- An understanding of how climate affects human activity, especially farming.

- Their knowledge of the British Empire and its legacy.

- Their understanding of the role of different employment sectors on the development of a country and how foreign investment might be involved.

A regional study of East Africa might therefore start by looking at its location, for – as Standish reminds us – all geography must start with "where" to give us a fixed point for further exploration.[11] Once this fixed point has been established, pupils could look at the region through each of the five lenses listed here: tectonic, development indicators, climate, history and employment, using what they learn to answer the overarching question.

Case study: Victoria Morris

There are three different types of place study that may be included in the primary geography curriculum:

1   A very brief introduction to the country's location and significant features at the point at which the country is mentioned in another context (for example, in a novel being read to a class). This would take only a small part of the lesson.

2   A brief study of the country (in, say, two to four lessons) before learning about it in another subject area, most likely in history.

3   A more in-depth study of the country, comprising a full-length geography unit of work. This would be the country selected to meet the "place knowledge" objective – a contrasting non-European country for Key Stage 1, or a European and North or South American country for Key Stage 2.

---

11 Standish, Geography, p. 89

I'm going to describe the process of planning a place study that could fit the final two options.

Firstly, we need to make sure that we've selected the right countries. With limited space in the curriculum, it's important to get the most value out of the countries we choose to focus on. Are your chosen countries the ones that your children, in your school, most need to know about in depth? There are several factors that you can evaluate to help you answer this question, including your pupils' backgrounds, the diversity in the local area and the human and physical features present in the local area. You can also consider countries that have a particularly interesting combination of human and physical features.

Once the countries have been selected, there are three questions I would ask in order to plan the knowledge to be taught in the unit.

1. Which national curriculum objectives can we meet?

Identify the main features of the country, focusing on what's asked for in the national curriculum. For Key Stage 2:

- Location – hemisphere, continent, capital, borders, coasts (on which oceans or seas?) and environmental regions.

- Physical – rivers, mountains, volcanoes and earthquakes, climate zones, biomes (including weather, landscape, flora and fauna) and vegetation belts.

- Human – types of settlement and land use, economic activity (industry), trade and natural resources (including energy, food, minerals and water) (and I'd add population and population density).

Once you know the facts, look for links and points of significance. So, for example, I'd look at the longest river – how important is it in the contexts of the country, the continent and the world? Why? This will often provide links to elements of human geography – such as water supply, industry, transporting natural resources, and using fertile land for agriculture. Thoroughly research these features of the country until you have a balanced overview and understand the interrelationships.

I choose to focus on the national curriculum objectives first, because this means that the place study will support the children's acquisition of geographical knowledge throughout the rest of the key stage. Also, it's easy to get sidetracked by things we find interesting when planning, and by starting in this way we are more likely to become interested in the features that our pupils need to learn about.

2. What's significant about this country?

Even if this is a longer unit, it's not going to be possible to cover all of the features mentioned here in depth. So, at this point, when we have identified all the knowledge that could be included, it is useful to consider what we would expect a child to know at the end of the unit. That the longest river in Norway is the Glomma, or that Norway has fjords? That wooden furniture is produced in the north of Italy, or that it is one of the few European countries with active volcanoes? If the country was Canada, I might focus on the timber industry, which I probably wouldn't do if the country was Mexico. This approach will help you decide what knowledge to teach, and in how much depth.

3. How does this unit build on prior learning and prepare for future learning?

Finally, I would select content carefully so that the unit fits well within the school's curriculum. If the pupils have already learnt about the different types of biome, I'd compare the biomes in the case study country in much more depth than if they hadn't. If they've already learnt about rivers, they should be able to use much more sophisticated vocabulary to describe them. However, just because they haven't yet learnt about something – let's say volcanoes – that doesn't mean that I would avoid the topic of volcanoes if they are a significant feature of the country that warrants discussion. I'd introduce them briefly, which has the added advantage that the pupils will already have some examples that they can recall when they do go on to learn about volcanoes.

Victoria Morris is a primary teacher and history and geography lead in Tower Hamlets. She tweets as @MrsSTeaches.

Place at GCSE

The thorough study of place at GCSE presents its own problems, one of which being that detailed regional studies are not encouraged by a fragmented specification that sticks fairly resolutely to a thematic approach. In her analysis of the latest reforms of the geography GCSE in England, Rawling notes that there was the potential to study place in a way that moved beyond a purely descriptive approach and instead took into account social-constructionist and phenomenological approaches.[12] She points to the requirement from the Department for Education that pupils must study:

> **the UK as a country and draw across physical and human characteristics to summarise significant geographical features and issues.[13]**

However, Rawling acknowledges that none of the approved specifications took on the challenge to create a regional approach to studying the UK and, despite what the titles of some units might suggest ("Living in the UK today" from the OCR Geography A specification or "UK Geographical Issues" from the Edexcel Geography B specification), the UK continues to be approached from a series of distinct themed perspectives, with little layering of the lenses that would allow pupils a deeper understanding of the complexity of place.

In the GCSE specifications, places tend to be used to exemplify very particular things. Pupils are called upon to use examples to show their knowledge of how

---

12 Rawling, Place in geography.
13 Department for Education, *Geography: GCSE Subject Content*. Ref: DFE-00345-2014 (2014), p. 6. Available at: https://assets.publishing.service.gov.uk/government/uploads/system/uploads/attachment_data/file/301253/GCSE_geography.pdf.

certain theoretical knowledge applies in practice. For example, the AQA specification asks that pupils learn:

> **An example of a small scale UK ecosystem to illustrate the concept of inter-relationships within a natural system, an understanding of producers, consumers, decomposers, food chain, food web and nutrient cycling.**[14]

The place chosen to exemplify this small-scale UK ecosystem is never referred to again in the specification and there is no expectation that it should be in the classroom either.

As well as these examples, the specifications also call for consideration of more detailed case studies in which a number of key ideas are explored. This brings us a little closer to a regional study of place, but in practice the key ideas are limited to a very narrow field. For example, the AQA specification calls for a case study of a tropical rainforest but only for it to be studied in terms of deforestation (causes, impacts and management). There is no suggestion that the places where tropical rainforests are found might be of geographical interest for any other reason, and so once again a simple story is told.

More detailed case studies are found in AQA's "Urban issues and challenges" and "The changing economic world" units in paper 2, in which two cities and two countries are studied in enough depth for them to almost become true place studies. The cities need to be studied in terms of a number of lenses, including migration, history, resource management, sustainability and employment structures. The country studies need to be viewed through the lenses of cultural, political and social geography (approaching Rawling's call for a social-constructionist approach), sustainability, globalisation, development studies and industrial development. Here too there are opportunities to apply geographical models, such as the demographic transition model, to real places and so help to develop pupils' procedural knowledge of the discipline.

We can see then that GCSE specifications do give some allowances for more detailed place studies but that they tend to rely to a greater extent on place to simply exemplify particular key ideas in a way that is likely to lead to a fragmented

---

14 AQA, *GCSE Geography (8035): Specification for Teaching from September 2016 Onward for Exams in 2018 Onwards* (2016), p. 12. Available at: https://filestore.aqa.org.uk/resources/geography/specifications/AQA-8035-SP-2016.PDF.

understanding of the discipline. However, as discussed in Chapter 2, the exam specifications are not the curriculum. There is room for us to approach things slightly differently to give place a more prominent position.

One way in which to do this is to make the links between Key Stage 3 and Key Stage 4 clearer and plan across them as a five-year curriculum. For example, if we know that pupils are going to look at tropical rainforests simply in terms of deforestation as part of their GCSE, you could look at said rainforests with a broader focus in Key Stage 3. This could be achieved by moving the GCSE case study from the often-used Amazon to an example from South Asia. This would give them the opportunity to look at the issue of tropical rainforests in a way that takes them beyond the simple headline of "deforestation" and towards a greater understanding of how they affect people, as well as how people affect them.

A similar approach could be taken when choosing the example of a small-scale UK ecosystem. I would suggest that in an ideal world this would be part of the "small area of the UK" looked at in Key Stage 1. This, however, would require an unprecedented amount of cooperation between primary and secondary schools in curriculum planning. Even at Key Stage 3, though, there should be space in the curriculum to look at a local area, perhaps as part of fieldwork in which pupils look at the various geographical processes affecting a local place (see Chapter 6).

A second way to approach it would be to combine case studies and examples in the GCSE specification so that the same places are looked at in different ways. For example, sticking with the AQA specification for now, we could study the region of West Africa and draw out:

- An example of a low-income country or newly emerging economy for "The changing economic world" unit (e.g. Nigeria).

- An example of a small-scale scheme for the sustainable supply of food/water/energy (e.g. stone lines for areas at risk of desertification in northern Nigeria, WaterAid working to supply wells and pumps, use of fuel-efficient stoves for energy conservation).

- An example of tourism linked to development (e.g. the difficulties faced by Gabon in developing tourism).

- A case study of a city in a low-income country or newly emerging economy (e.g. Lagos).

- An example of planning to help the urban poor (e.g. informal housing improvements in Lagos).

- An example of desertification (e.g. in northern Nigeria).

- A tropical rainforest case study (e.g. deforestation for cocoa plantations).

Such an approach will create challenges – there are not yet textbooks or commercial resources designed with this approach in mind – but it will also create the opportunity for pupils to develop a much greater understanding of what geographers mean when they talk about places and how they create geographical knowledge by applying these different lenses to those places. Their knowledge will be that much more powerful.

Case study: David Preece

Loved and hated in equal measure, it's hard to imagine an understanding of geography that isn't grounded in specific placed examples. Used to illustrate ideas, to exemplify concepts, or to better understand the operation of a process, the humble case study is inherently and intrinsically associated with the discipline of geography, and with our teaching of it at all levels. But how do we choose where to focus?

Sometimes, the approach is primarily pragmatic. Resource availability – whether that be good quality articles, images, DVDs or mapping introductions – can be critical for our ability to explore a sense of place with our pupils. In a busy environment, in which teachers do not have the luxury of large amounts of time to research multiple options and then select and present the best one, often the pragmatic considerations of "What have we got?" or "What have we taught before?" or "What good DVDs have we got?" will take precedence. These are understandable, but perhaps not the most geographical, reasons for choosing a case study, and can often lead to slightly clichéd interpretations. Geography teacher Jo Payne talks powerfully about Bangladesh being used to illustrate the causes and impacts of flooding, for instance, whilst pupils learn little about the wider country, the context or the geography.[15] Bangladesh's

---

15 For more on this, see John Hopkin, Sampling the world, *Teaching Geography* 36(3) (2011): 96–97.

flooding is isolated and decontextualised – it becomes a single story for learners.[16]

When selecting and thinking about my examples, I am inherently apprehensive about using textbook case studies for this reason: the over-reliance on the single narrative – plus the fact that a significant number of other pupils will be using the exact same case study – makes me concerned for the geography that I am teaching. Too often, as a GCSE and A level examiner, you see the same factual recall trotted out – bearing almost no relevance to the question – and it becomes a real joy to find a pupil who can articulately explore and understand the relevance of place-specific details in a new case study. There is, too, the risk of familiarity – you would have to write something incredible to stand out amidst a sea of Bangladesh flooding examples – whilst more innovative case studies can help candidates float a bit higher.

The counterpoint to this approach is to insist that case studies are "chosen from the 21st century" – as if relative modernity will counterbalance the risk of cliché. This is well-intentioned, I'm sure, with the aim of connecting pupils to events that have happened within their lifetime, or that they may personally remember. But here, too, I am wary. A poor example from when a pupil is two years old is far less powerful than a well-chosen, well-resourced and superbly explained example from before they were born: the quality of the teaching is how you strengthen the connection, and help pupils to understand the importance and expression of place. For me, the story of what happened – and how that has led to long-term change in behaviour or management – is vital. I have long argued for a deeply contextualised case study approach that includes temporal context. Personally, I still teach the 1995 Kobe earthquake as part of a longer-term view that explores how the evolution of Japanese earthquake management is ongoing: the changes from Kobe are connected directly to the lifesaving advances implemented in the Sendai quake. And, similarly, failures to adequately prepare for the secondary hazards can be contextualised in the journey from Kobe, and understood better as a cyclical hazard management technique that constantly seeks to improve upon identified weaknesses.

Many of the contemporary case studies that teachers choose – taking the news into the classroom – fail to take account of the longer-term context that is

16 Biddulph, Editorial: "the danger of a single story".

required to really understand hazard management. While it might be great to look at the news reports (because the resources are readily available), we can't possibly understand the longer-term effects of an event that's a week or two old. Look at the 2010 Haiti earthquake: it's only through that long-term lens that the full horrors of post-colonial legacy, the reliance on non-governmental organisations (NGOs) and the complex failures of governance are fully and truly understood. As a form tutor, perhaps, I'd want to explore what's going on in the world; as a geography teacher, my pupils deserve a more rigorous academic grounding of their case study material, and I am happy to pick older examples.

Finally, as we are increasingly conscious of cognitive load, and of the teaching time we have available, it is often helpful to select case study examples that cover multiple dimensions. Whilst there is a risk of "the wrong bit" being discussed, I'd argue strongly that pupils enjoy a better sense of place when they see the case study from multiple perspectives, and see it a number of times. We look, for instance, at the regeneration of London from multiple perspectives: the decline and deindustrialisation phase, the urban decline and challenge phase, and the regeneration of the London Docklands and Stratford Olympic region, and the ways in which these components are connected and threaded together. We might explore these places at multiple points in our GCSE course, and come back to them as contrasting examples for A level, ensuring our pupils have the opportunity to explore the depth and layers of landscape context from a number of angles, and build a stronger sense of place.

And, ultimately, isn't that what we want from the case study experience?

David Preece is an experienced head of geography in south-east London. He tweets as @DoctorPreece.

Questions

- Review the current places being used as case studies in your curriculum. What is the rationale for their inclusion?

- Which different geographical themes could be used to explore a single place in your programme of study?

- Can you think of occasions when a single story is told about a place in your curriculum?

Further reading

Eleanor Rawling, Place in geography: change and challenge. In Mark Jones and David Lambert (eds), *Debates in Geography Education*, 2nd edn (Abingdon and New York: Routledge, 2018), pp. 49–61.

Alex Standish, The place of regional geography. In Mark Jones and David Lambert (eds), *Debates in Geography Education*, 2nd edn (Abingdon and New York: Routledge, 2018), pp. 62–74.

Chapter 8

Sequencing the curriculum

The discipline of geography has a horizontal structure, which can mean we end up with quite shallow knowledge of a wide range of topics. A geographer might be expected to know a little about the processes of glaciation, the rise of megacities and the consequences of climate change. This can, if we are not careful, lead to a fragmented school curriculum in which pupils study these different topics under the heading of "geography" without anything explicit to tie them together.

One factor that often exacerbates this problem is the way in which curricula build up and develop over time. As we saw in Part I, a new national curriculum can be introduced at the whim of government. We have had five different versions of the Key Stage 3 national curriculum, and four versions for Key Stages 1 and 2, since 1991. Geography departments could choose to throw out their old programmes of study and start again from scratch, but this would be a huge undertaking. Instead, what is more likely is that there will be some alterations to the existing programme, with a topic being removed to make way for the demands of the new national curriculum, or a topic simply being given a new focus. Curricular revisions may also be occasioned by the appointment of a new head of department or by the school's changing priorities.

Whilst it is understandable that a school's geography curriculum may evolve in this way, it does not make it any less problematic in terms of the purpose being lost or confused during each revision. You increasingly end up with a curriculum comprised of disparate topics, each acting as a silo of information, with nothing connecting them and little deep rationale for their inclusion.

The table that follows shows a fairly standard Key Stage 3 programme of study. It is entirely typical of those found in schools I have worked in or visited over the years.

Year 7	Year 8	Year 9
Using maps	Geography of sport	Rainforests
Our local area	Development	Work and industry
Uganda	Urbanisation	Tectonics
Cold environments	Coasts	Sustainable fashion
Rivers	Migration	Globalisation
Weather and climate	Climate change	Geography of disease

Looking back now, some of its features seem obviously flawed. Firstly, the fact that there are six topics in each year is a common feature in many schools, often arranged that way so that an assessment can be carried out at the end of each half term. However, this would suggest that for some reason the study of each topic takes exactly one half term, regardless of how many weeks comprise that half term or how much pupils need to know about the topic.

Secondly, some of the choices seem, on the surface, to be somewhat arbitrary. Uganda was included because the school had links to a charity working there and the geography department were told that they needed to introduce the pupils to the country in Year 7. Likewise, work and industry was included in Year 9 to meet the school's demands that subjects show links to careers education. Geography of sport was included at the start of Year 8 as there were concerns about the behaviour of some of the boys and it was hoped that this would engage them. The sustainable fashion unit in Year 9 was a similar incentive designed to motivate disengaged girls.

Thirdly, the sequencing makes little sense. The study of Uganda rightly belongs after the development unit in Year 8, but this was already in place. It would make more sense to look at weather and climate before studying cold environments, but the department wanted to do some fieldwork around weather and this is easier, and more pleasant, to do in the summer term. There are many such examples in this programme of study, mostly because each topic is being treated in isolation, with little thought regarding the wider journey through the curriculum. We are simply ticking off topics that pupils are expected to have studied whilst doing something with the umbrella term "geography".

There is an alternative to this silo model of curriculum design and that is to adopt a tapestry model, in which we see our curriculum as being made up of many threads that weave together to reveal the big picture: the whole being greater than the sum of its parts. The tapestry model means that nothing stands in isolation and everything studied becomes relevant and *powerful*. The aim of this model is to ensure that we are explicit about where pupils will revisit previous ideas and apply them again in the future. This uses well-established ideas of retrieval practice, spacing and interleaving, as well as schema development.

Revisiting, retrieving and spacing

The idea that returning to the object of study is important is not new; indeed, it has been explored by researchers since at least the 19th century. Hermann Ebbinghaus studied how long it took to forget nonsense syllables that he had memorised and found there was a steep forgetting curve. Once studied they were quickly forgotten. However, he also found that if he revisited them it took longer for him to forget. Every time he went back to them, he remembered them for a little longer. His lesson is that if we want to remember something, we need to come back to it frequently.[1]

If we look at the table on page 112 in light of this, we can see that there is a problem: it does not encourage this kind of frequent revisiting. Pupils learn how to use maps at the start of Year 7 but may not practise this again until Year 10 or 11. They study cold environments in the spring of Year 7 but the topics that follow don't return to them. To take advantage of the power of the forgetting curve we need to build in opportunities for pupils to use those map skills again in future topics. If they are going to study cold environments, they need to use what they have learnt again and again.

This could be done within the existing structure. Cold environments could be revisited when looking at climate change in Year 8. Pupils could be asked to explain how a changing climate could affect the cold environments which they

---

1 Hermann Ebbinghaus, *Memory: A Contribution to Experimental Psychology*, trs Henry A. Ruger and Clara E. Bussenius (New York: Teachers College, Columbia University 1913 [1885]).

studied. They could revisit this knowledge again when studying rainforests – for example, by contrasting the water cycle in the Arctic tundra and the tropics.

The same could be done with the use of maps. Their Ordnance Survey map-reading skills could be deployed in a study of rivers to help them trace the route of a river and comment on the changing landscape as we follow the long profile. They could also use these maps to identify how urban areas have changed over time and to describe settlement patterns. They could use cartographic data to describe the spread of diseases in the geography of disease unit or to show development indicators when looking at development.

It is worth pointing out that some of this interweaving might happen anyway. It is difficult to envision a geography class *not* looking at a choropleth map showing variations of gross national income (GNI) per capita, or coming across data displayed on a map, in their other topics. What we are looking for, however, is a very explicit link back to previous learning and the expectation that pupils draw directly on what they have learnt in order to access what comes next. This is because as well as there being strong curricular reasons to revisit previous topics there are also pedagogical considerations.

We know that there is a difference between restudying something you previously learnt and retrieving it from memory. A review of the evidence by researchers Jeffrey Karpicke and Phillip Grimaldi show that pupils remember much less when asked to restudy something than when they are asked to recall it.[2] This has led to a rise in the use of retrieval practice – for example, through regular quizzing or homework tasks. It also means that when we revisit an idea in a different context, we want to draw on pupils' memories of it in the previous topic, rather than presenting it as something to be studied again. For example, if we are going to ask them to use what they learnt about cold environments to predict how a changing climate will affect these regions, we want pupils to access their memories. We don't want to end up reteaching the material in a different guise.

---

2   Jeffrey D. Karpicke and Phillip J. Grimaldi, Retrieval-based learning: a perspective for enhancing meaningful learning, *Educational Psychology Review* 24(3) (2012): 401–418.

In practice, this could involve a task like this:

Context: We have looked at how global temperatures are rising over time. Last year you looked at cold environments, such as those of Russia's Arctic tundra. Think back to that topic and consider the following questions:

- Why was the flow of water very slow in the Arctic? What will happen if temperatures rise?

- How have animals adapted to the cold environment? How will temperature rises leave them unprepared?

- Why is there little vegetation growth in the Arctic? How might warming temperatures affect this?

- Why might changing patterns of vegetation in the Arctic help to solve some of the problems of warming temperatures?

As long as your questions cover material that you taught pupils in their topic on cold environments, they should be able to answer them from memory. It might be that some pupils need a few prompts, such as a climate graph or images of animals from the area, but really we want them to understand that they are being asked to apply knowledge from one topic to another to strengthen their schema. This will help them to not only remember what they were taught for longer but also to develop their understanding of how geographers approach knowledge across diverse fields.

Interweaving threads

As I have mentioned, one way to ensure that concepts are frequently revisited is to see them as the threads that weave together to form the tapestry of your curriculum. These threads may be thematic (climate, tectonics, hydrology, etc.) or they could be places that will be used to illustrate these themes at different points over the years. Other threads may be geographical skills, and procedural and disciplinary knowledge, that pupils will use, return to and improve. These threads on their own might seem somewhat inconsequential but together they create something greater than the sum of their parts: they allow us to create the big picture of *geography* itself.

Let us consider how this might look in practice with an example of how several threads could come together throughout a selection of topics in Key Stage 3.

Thread 1: thematic – tectonics

Early on in Key Stage 3 pupils are introduced to the theory of plate tectonics. They look at how the movement of plates creates hazards and how countries at different levels of development manage them. Later in the same key stage they study East Africa as a piece of regional geography and consider how physical geography has shaped people's lives. As part of this they look at the Great Rift Valley: its formation through tectonic processes and its impacts on people.

They look again at how tectonic landscapes affect people when they consider their own local landscape (in this case, the Weald) and how it was shaped through uplift and then erosion through the different rock layers.

This tectonic thread re-emerges in a later topic when they study Haiti and answer the fertile question "Why is Haiti the least economically developed country in the western hemisphere?" (for more on fertile questions see Chapter 9). Here they consider whether physical geography (e.g. its tectonic position) or human geography has done the most to hold it back.

Thread 2: thematic – development

Pupils start Key Stage 3 by contrasting two countries which are at different levels of economic development: the UK and Uganda. They are introduced to the idea of development indicators as a method of comparing countries and to the idea that development is more than economic.

When they move on to look at plate tectonics and how countries manage hazards, they use development indicators to see whether development has an effect on the damage caused by earthquakes and volcanic eruptions.

This thread is also used in their regional study of East Africa, in which they consider how the region has been portrayed in the past and whether this portrayal is still accurate. They also contrast the development levels of countries within the region, using some of the same techniques they developed in their first topic.

When they come to look at Haiti they first use the thread of development to understand the country's development in a regional context before considering the different barriers to development and testing which might be most significant.

Thread 3: procedural – choropleth maps

Geographers are interested in spatial variations, and one way in which such variations are shown is using maps. Throughout these topics, pupils are introduced to a wide range of cartographic displays of data and taught how to interpret them. Importantly, these same types of displays are used again in the future.

When they study development in contrasting parts of the world at the start of the key stage, they look at choropleth maps showing global variations in GNI per capita. They create their own choropleth maps to show other development indicators and then use them to identify patterns. They also learn the limitations of these choropleth maps by considering the ways in which they disguise variation *within* a country.

When they study East Africa, the same maps are referred back to in order to contrast development both within the region and between different areas. They use the same type of map to study variations in climate and to help explain population distribution in the region.

Thread 4: place – Haiti

We have already seen that Haiti is a place where at least two threads – tectonics and development – can come together, but places can also provide threads that run through the curriculum.

Images of the aftermath of Haiti's 2010 earthquake could be used in the tectonics topic to show the secondary impacts of hazards. Haiti could also be used as a case study in the weather and climate topic when pupils are learning about the formation of hurricanes or the features of a tropical climate. They could come across Haiti again when looking at the impacts of deforestation, with images to contrast it with its neighbour, the Dominican Republic. If this was done well, by the time they came to study Haiti towards the end of the key stage, pupils would already have a good knowledge of it as a place and the challenges it faces.

The same approach can be taken with any key stage and can (and *should*) be taken across key stages. The aim is always the same: to use and build on what has come before so as to make the curriculum a tapestry model.

One thing after another – looking back

Identifying threads that run through our curriculum is a vital first step, but it is only of use if it is followed by further action. Once we have identified the threads, we need to use them to ensure that we are always looking back at what has come before and preparing pupils for what comes later. There are a number of practical steps we can take to ensure that this happens.

Quiz it

Perhaps the most common way to look back at content is through quizzing. The power of retrieval practice to ensure that what is studied can be retained and used in the future is well established. As a result, it is becoming increasingly common to see lessons beginning with some form of quiz of previous learning, often with questions drawn from a mixture of random content from previous terms, previous weeks and previous lessons.

One simple alteration we can make is to give more thought to the choice of content. Rather than choosing questions at random, or due to how long it has been since the material was first studied, we can choose them because they relate in some way to what is being studied next. Pupils may be studying a region in North America in Key Stage 2 and be about to look at the way in which the climate changes as you move across the landmass from the sea. They might therefore begin with a quiz on what they learnt about relief rainfall a couple of years before. This not only has the benefit of retrieval practice making this easier to recall again in the future, but also helps to develop their schema by enabling them to link what they are about to learn about the climate across a region to what they already know about the causes of such patterns.

Question it

It is also possible to make the links between different topics explicit through our use of questioning in class. For example, pupils might be studying Lagos as a case study of a city in a low-income country or newly emerging economy that experiences both opportunities and challenges. They may have already studied Nigeria as a case study of a country with a changing economy. This gives us opportunities to ask questions during the Lagos topic that refer back to their work on Nigeria. These might include things like:

- How does desertification in northern Nigeria create problems for Lagos in the south?

- What else might be driving migration from the northern areas to cities like Lagos?

- How is Nigeria's employment structure changing?

- How might these changes be driven by growth in Lagos?

- Why might Lagos experience water scarcity despite its high levels of rainfall?

These questions draw not only from pupils' current unit on Lagos but also from the previous one on Nigeria and, if they have already studied the topics, on previous work on water management and hot deserts.

One problem with questioning in the classroom is that, unlike a quiz, you may only have the person who is asked the question actively trying to retrieve the information from their long-term memory, whilst the rest of the class sits back and waits. Indeed, research from Magdalena Abel and Henry Roediger found that pupils who hear an answer given by a classmate receive little benefit in terms of their own ability to recall the answer in the future.[3] They just do not need to think hard enough. A potential solution is to get into the habit of asking the question, pausing

---

3   Magdalena Abel and Henry L. Roediger III, The testing effect in a social setting: does retrieval practice benefit a listener?, *Journal of Experimental Psychology: Applied* 24(3) (2018): 347–359.

for everyone to think of an answer, and only then selecting a pupil to answer it. Hopefully, this will lead to everyone doing the thinking.

Picture it

An easy way in which to highlight the links between different topics is to use recurring images. If pupils are going to study a particular place in depth, then images of that place could be used in prior thematic topics. For example, if they are going to study Haiti, expose them to images of that place when studying:

- Impacts of earthquakes.

- Tropical climates.

- Informal housing.

- Human rights abuses.

- The impact of trade subsidies.

- Deforestation.

These same images can also be used across thematic topics. For example, if pupils have studied informal housing when looking at urbanisation, you could use the same image of this informal housing when looking at the impacts of earthquakes. The images used to show deforestation when looking at ecosystems might also be used to show how this deforestation increases the risk of landslides following an earthquake.

Hopefully, seeing the same images again will trigger memories of their use in another context, especially if combined with the quizzing and questioning techniques discussed in this chapter.

Review it

Pupils will benefit from regular opportunities to review what they have previously learnt as it gives them the chance to view it in light of subsequent knowledge. As an example, at GCSE level, a review lesson looking back at the 2015 Nepal earthquake – first studied several weeks ago – could encourage pupils to think about it in terms of what they now know about Typhoon Haiyan or the pressures caused by rapid urbanisation. In this way, pupils make those important links between topics that are not immediately apparent in a fragmented specification.

This kind of review can be conducted in a number of ways. It could be through dedicated lessons, built into lesson time, or take place as regular homework activities. It can also be useful to carry out such a review one-to-one by sitting down with a pupil and discussing their previous work with them. This gives you a chance to ask questions and draw their attention to ways in which topics connect. One way to achieve this is to set aside time to talk with one pupil per lesson whilst everyone else works independently on a task.

Putting the sequence together

Getting our curriculum sequence right is vitally important. One way to approach the task is to write all the topics you have decided to study on sticky notes and then move them around until you are happy with the order. If you can do this as a department, or as a group of subject leaders working across schools, then so much the better. It is a good opportunity to discuss the thinking behind the sequence you suggest and to see how it differs from everyone else's ideas.

Once you have an order that you think works, place the sticky notes in a circle on a large piece of paper, working clockwise around the key stage. Next, start drawing lines between the topics to show the links and annotate the lines to explain what they are. For example, you might have a line running between the topics of climate and Haiti saying "Impact of tropical storms", or between climate change and Russia saying "Impact of melting sea ice on trade". Once this is done you can transfer the sequence into a table that lists both the order of the topics and the links between them. You could also use the planning template at the end of this book, which is designed to help you think about the knowledge in each topic and the ways in which each topic builds towards something bigger than itself. That happens when we start thinking about geography as an active process and is the topic of our next chapter.

Questions

- Think about the very first geography topic that you teach. Why do you start with this one? When will pupils encounter this topic again in the future?

- If you teach geography at Key Stages 4 and 5, to what extent do you feel like the specification has become the curriculum? To what extent do you think this is a problem?

- How could you make the connections between topics explicit to your pupils so that they see geography's big picture?

Further reading

Liz Taylor, Progression. In Mark Jones (ed.), *The Handbook of Secondary Geography* (Sheffield: The Geographical Association, 2017), pp. 40–47.

Clare Brooks, Understanding conceptual development in school geography. In Mark Jones and David Lambert (eds), *Debates in Geography Education*, 2nd edn (Abingdon and New York: Routledge, 2018), pp. 103–114.

Chapter 9

Doing geography

Sequencing our curriculum around the thematic topics and places being studied will only take us so far. If we are going to base our curriculum on the principles of powerful knowledge, we also need to consider how we develop a disciplinary understanding of the subject; we need pupils to know how we *do* geography. This ability is based on a combination of the propositional knowledge that a geographer brings to a problem *and* the procedural knowledge needed to address it. For example, if we wanted to investigate the way in which a river is behaving on a meander, we would need the propositional knowledge to form a hypothesis about what is happening (rates of erosion on the outside bend, rates of deposition on the inside bend, and how the geology and velocity is affecting the rate of movement) along with procedural knowledge about how to test that hypothesis (how to collect data on these things).

Overarching both the propositional and the procedural knowledge is the ability to *think geographically*, to see the world in a distinctly geographical way, which involves a deep understanding of the nature of the subject. This ability to think geographically may be taken for granted by a graduate of the subject who cannot do anything but view the world transformed by what they have learnt. This is exactly what a powerful education should achieve. We cannot stand on the summit of a mountain without reading the physical processes that shaped what we see. We cannot read an article about migration through North Africa without linking it to a wider view of the pressures on the region. We think geographically because we hold powerful knowledge of this subject. It can be hard to remember that our pupils will not automatically see the world in this way and need to be taught to do so. Like anything that needs to be taught, it becomes a curricular issue.

One of the problems we saw with a Future 2 curriculum was a rush towards *doing* before the required *knowing* had been secured. In part this was because of a belief that pupils would learn best from direct and authentic experience. This led to the creation of the now much-criticised "cone of learning", which lists a range of activities and purports to say how much pupils will retain from each one. It often looks something like this:

- Reading – 10%

- Audio-visual – 20%

- Demonstration – 30%

- Discussion – 50%

- Practice doing – 75%

- Teach others – 90%

These figures are usually attributed to the National Training Laboratories in Bethel, Maine, in the USA, but as Paul Kirschner and Carl Hendrick explain, when asked about the origin of the data, they can't provide a link to the research.[1] It appears to be a corruption of the work of Edgar Dale, who produced a taxonomy of how far different media strayed from direct experience – there was no mention of this affecting retention of information. Despite its dubious basis, the theory stuck, and teachers were urged to get pupils *doing* so that they would start learning.[2] The problem arises when pupils are moved towards doing or teaching others before they have the requisite knowledge with which to do or teach the thing. This is not to downplay the importance of direct experience in the curriculum, but just to emphasise that it needs to come at the right time. As with so much else, what might appear to be a pedagogical matter is also a matter of curriculum. When in the curriculum will pupils have opportunities to do geography and to practise thinking geographically?

There are a few distinctly geographical areas in which experience and learning tend to come to the fore: fieldwork, geographical enquiry and, increasingly, tools like GIS, the use of which might underpin both.

1   Paul A. Kirschner and Carl Hendrick, *How Learning Happens: Seminal Works in Educational Psychology and What They Mean in Practice* (Abingdon and New York: Routledge, 2020).
2   Mark Enser, Education myths: an origin story. In Craig Barton (ed.), *The researchED Guide to Education Myths: An Evidence-Informed Guide for Teachers* (Woodbridge: John Catt Educational, 2019), pp. 19–28.

Fieldwork

Fieldwork – or, at least, the field trip – is one of those things that the great British public seems to associate most with the subject of geography as they recollect their own school days. This is not surprising; we remember those things that break from routine. We can remember the day spent stood in the drizzle counting pedestrians moving towards a shopping centre, the anxiety of having to approach people with a questionnaire, the time we had to climb a steep shingle beach with a clinometer in hand. The day-to-day of classrooms, bells and pencil cases merges into one. That field trips are memorable can lead to us overstating their importance in and of themselves. The types of memories discussed here are *episodic* – memories of episodes in our lives – not necessarily ones that help us to build more powerful, abstract geographical knowledge. For that we need *semantic* memories. The trouble is that semantic memories are not attached to any particular event; we do not remember how we learnt what we know. But this is also their strength. Because they are not attached to any particular event, we can apply this abstract knowledge in a range of different situations.[3] What we want to do is ensure that field trips create not just episodic memories but semantic ones as well. We want to ensure that pupils actually learn some geography whilst they are there.

This brings us to what can be a useful distinction between field trips and fieldwork. Field trips are any activity undertaken outside of school. This might include a visit to a museum or a local place of worship, or a week in Iceland. The purposes of field trips may vary, but are usually about offering an experience of something different to the pupils' everyday lives. They create episodic memories. Fieldwork, in contrast, is concerned with using out-of-classroom experiences to do geography. The goal is not the experience itself but the geographical learning that emerges from it. This means that fieldwork needs to be built into the curriculum in a way that stand-alone field trips might not, as it should be embedded in what pupils are learning about in class. The work they do before and after becomes important in turning the experience into learning.

---

3 Clare Sealy, Memorable experiences are the best way to help children remember things. In Craig Barton (ed.), *The researchED Guide to Education Myths: An Evidence-Informed Guide for Teachers* (Woodbridge: John Catt Educational, 2019), pp. 29–40.

The link between the classroom and experience is made by educational researcher David Kolb in his work on the experiential learning cycle.[4] This cycle suggests that people need to combine experience with reflection, theory and experimentation in order to learn from it. Although originally based on the need to create a curriculum and assessment model for adult vocational education, there are clear applications to the geography curriculum and to fieldwork in particular. Kolb's cycle may look something like this:

Abstract conceptualisation
Classroom-based theory about the topic under investigation.

Reflective observation
Returning to the classroom to reflect on what was experienced.

Active experimentation
Forming a hypothesis and planning the investigation.

Concrete experience
Carrying out the investigation and gathering data in the field.

An example could involve a class starting with the abstract conceptualisation phase by studying the theory of urban inequalities and how they emerge. This will hopefully build on prior learning about urban areas and settlement patterns and draw on a wide range of contrasting places to show how distributions of inequality

4   David A. Kolb, *Experiential Learning: Experience as the Source of Learning and Development* (Upper Saddle River, NJ: Prentice Hall, 1983).

vary. The aim of this abstract conceptualisation is to give pupils a lens through which to see the world as they encounter it. They are creating semantic memories which can be applied to many different situations.

They then move on to the active experimentation phase and start to plan a geographical enquiry to see which factors have influenced inequalities in an urban area that they will visit. In this stage of the cycle, pupils are learning to think geographically and to consider how disciplinary knowledge is created. They will need to learn about issues of reliability and validity as well as the appropriate qualitative and quantitative research methods.

The next step would be for them to experience carrying out the enquiry: the fieldwork. Here they will be encouraged to apply the geographical lens they created during the abstract conceptualisation phase and to be aware of their surroundings. They will be carrying out the research methodology they planned in the active experimentation phase and, again, need to be reminded to focus not just on the data they are gathering but on the process of gathering it.

Finally, and importantly, pupils need time for reflection: to reflect on the theories they started with and to consider how their own experience supports or challenges these ideas. They will also reflect on their data collection methodology, and the potential flaws with their methods. This should better enable them to understand the critiques of geographical research that they encounter.

We can see how this process plays out in the non-examined assessment (NEA) that makes up part of the A level course. The table that follows shows how elements of the mark scheme, in this case from OCR, link with the stages of the experiential learning cycle.

Stages of Kolb's experiential learning cycle	Aspects of the OCR NEA mark scheme[5]
Abstract conceptualisation	The plan is based on an individual geographical topic or issue, which is accurately and appropriately defined and within a research framework.

5   OCR, OCR A Level Geography H481/04/05 Investigative Geography Mark Recording Sheet (2019). Available at: https://www.ocr.org.uk/Images/349152-a-level-mark-recording-sheet.pdf.

Stages of Kolb's experiential learning cycle	Aspects of the OCR NEA mark scheme
	There is clear evidence of valid and individual literature research that defines and contextualises the investigation through an appropriate combination of wider geographical links, comparisons, models and theory. The range of data presentation techniques is appropriate and well selected, with good knowledge and understanding of the relevant techniques for representing results clearly. There is effective use of appropriate knowledge, theory and geographical concepts to help explain findings.
Active experimentation	There is a clear, well focused plan, appropriately designed to include aims or questions or hypotheses linked to the geographic purpose of the investigation. The plan is based on an individual geographical topic or issue, which is accurately and appropriately defined and within a research framework.
Concrete experience	There is clear evidence of personalised methodologies and approaches to observe and record primary data and phenomena in the field and to incorporate secondary data and/or evidence, collected individually or in groups. There is clear evidence of the ability to collect and use digital, geo-located data.
Reflective observation	There is convincing evidence that conducting the investigation extended geographical understanding with clear reference to the wider geographical context of the investigation.

Stages of Kolb's experiential learning cycle	Aspects of the OCR NEA mark scheme
	There is a strong evaluation of the overall success of the investigation with reference to the reliability of data sources, data collection methods (including sampling), the accuracy of data collected and the extent to which it is representative, and the validity of the analysis and conclusions.

Fieldwork is generally seen as a Good Thing by geography teachers, but it can be a mistake to think of it as being a powerful part of geography in and of itself. As with so much else, it is what you do with it that counts. A report by the National Foundation for Education Research (NFER) concludes that for fieldwork to be effective it needs to be:[6]

●   Properly conceived. Thought needs to go into the purpose of the fieldwork and this purpose needs to influence the form it takes. The role of both the teacher and the pupil needs to be considered.

●   Adequately planned. From risk assessments to the equipment needed (and available), we need to plan out how the logistics of the fieldwork will operate.

●   Well taught. As discussed, pupils will not necessarily learn powerful geography simply from being outside the classroom; there will always be an element of direction and guidance. On top of this they need to be taught how to conduct an investigation.

●   Effectively followed up. They need that time for reflection after the fieldwork to link what they saw in the field to what they learnt in the classroom. They also need opportunities to revisit what they learnt (see below).

There are a few considerations we need to make when planning fieldwork as part of our curriculum. Primarily, we need to ensure that our fieldwork aligns with our

6   Mark Rickinson, Justin Dillon, Kelly Teamey, Marian Morris, Mee Young Choi, Dawn Sanders and Pauline Benefield, *A Review of Research on Outdoor Learning* (Slough: National Foundation for Education Research and King's College London, 2014).

curriculum's purpose. If, as this book suggests, we accept that the purpose of the curriculum is to develop powerful geographical knowledge in our pupils, then our fieldwork should be a way of putting this into practice. This might mean rethinking excursions that are field trips, rather than true fieldwork, so that experiences are transformed into geographical understanding.

Another reason why we should rethink field trips is the issue of equality. One key tenet of powerful knowledge is that everyone is entitled to the same education. Field trips can be expensive, with visits to popular places like Iceland, Italy or New York running into hundreds of pounds. This becomes an opportunity for the few rather than education for all. The time that a teacher spends on organising and running a trip for a few pupils is time they are not spending on the education of everyone else. Time is a valuable resource and we need to spend it well.

So we need to think of fieldwork as we would any other part of the curriculum: in terms of its sequencing, content and place.

Sequencing

The same principles apply to placing fieldwork in the curriculum as they do to anything else we want our pupils to learn. There is little point in introducing a class to a particular method of data collection during a piece of Year 7 fieldwork if you are not going to return to it again. It will simply be forgotten. For example, if pupils start learning how to use quadrats as part of a systematic sampling technique to investigate the effects of footfall on biodiversity, they will need to revisit:

- The propositional knowledge regarding the links between human activity and biodiversity.

- The procedural knowledge of how to carry out their own survey of biodiversity.

- The wider disciplinary knowledge of the importance of sampling techniques.

This does not mean that they necessarily need to carry out fieldwork based on these areas again, but they will need to re-encounter them in the classroom and be reminded of what they did in the field.

We also need to consider where the fieldwork belongs in the learning sequence: whether you start with it (the concrete experience in Kolb's experiential learning cycle) or with the theory (the abstract conceptualisation). There are arguments in favour of both.

You might decide to start with the experience so as to avoid the criticism that can be directed at much school-level fieldwork: that the end result of the investigation is already known to all concerned.[7] For example, pupils might go to the coast to investigate the way in which groynes interrupt the flow of longshore drift. However, if they have studied longshore drift in the classroom, they already know exactly what they will find. They might go through the process of carrying out an investigation without really being engaged in it as there is no *need to know* – no curiosity that has been inspired in them.

However, this approach requires us to believe that the purpose of fieldwork is to create new propositional knowledge, at least for the pupils carrying it out. In our longshore drift example, the fieldwork is being done so that they learn how groynes affect the flow of sediment along the coast. This is a very inefficient way of building new knowledge. A teacher and a whiteboard, possibly aided with a video clip, could ensure that pupils had this knowledge in five minutes, compared to a whole day spent at the coast. There is also a risk that by putting experience before abstract knowledge, pupils will develop misconceptions. Perhaps their measurements are off, and they learn that there is more deposition downdrift. Or they might conclude from their data not that deposition is taking place and leading to a higher beach updrift but, rather, that the land must be eroding away downdrift to make it lower.

What we can do is ensure that pupils are already knowledgeable about what they will find before the fieldwork, then focus not on *what* geographers know but on *how* they know it. We want them to be aware of the potential pitfalls of different data collection methods and why results may not always be reliable or the data valid for the conclusions we are trying to draw. We also want them to see the ways in which what they learn in the classroom may be more nuanced in the real world than the textbooks would suggest. This is far more difficult to do in the classroom.

---

7   John Widdowson and Alan Parkinson, *Fieldwork Through Enquiry* (Sheffield: The Geographical Association, 2013).

Content

The same kind of thinking needs to go into selecting the content for fieldwork as goes into the rest of the curriculum. However, with fieldwork you are likely to also be constrained by the practicalities of your location. I would dearly love to carry out some fieldwork on the lasting legacy of glaciation on upland areas of the UK, but from our location in Sussex it is unlikely that my school would be able to run this in a way that would be accessible to all our pupils.

There are two possible ways to approach the selection of fieldwork opportunities. The first is to start with the classroom-based curriculum and look for opportunities to include fieldwork within it. For example, you might decide that you could include a microclimate investigation within the weather and climate topic you have planned, or investigate the impact of different forms of agriculture on biodiversity when studying food resources. An alternative approach is to begin with the fieldwork and ensure that you are planning the opportunities to teach the abstract conceptualisation that will support it. So, you might not have planned to teach food resources at Key Stage 2, but then realise that you have an opportunity to carry out an investigation on nearby farmland and so plan a topic around it.

In practice, most teachers will adopt a combination of approaches. What is important is that the consideration is there when you start planning so these opportunities are embedded into the curriculum, not an afterthought. Trying to retrofit fieldwork into the existing curriculum will mean that it is likely to fall into the trap highlighted by the NFER report and will not be properly conceived of, planned, taught or followed up.

Place

Finally, we need to give some thought to where we chose to conduct our fieldwork. Again, this will always depend somewhat on location, and fieldwork will often happen in the school grounds or immediate surroundings. These opportunities should not be overlooked or seen as less important than visits to unfamiliar places, as this way the focus can really be on developing disciplinary skills and understanding, rather than attempting to build new propositional knowledge about somewhere new. For example, an investigation into the microclimate around the school site can mean that pupils think hard about how to reduce the risk of collecting unreliable data, rather than about exploring a place that is new to them.

Sometimes, however, we will have the opportunity to travel further afield. When that is the case, we need to think about the points discussed in Chapter 7 and ensure that we don't end up telling a simple story about that place. It is all too easy for pupils to only encounter a neighbourhood as somewhere used to typify social deprivation and to miss everything else that makes that place what it is. The same pitfalls can apply to those exciting, seemingly geographical opportunities to take pupils to far-flung places where they actually learn little more than "Iceland is the land of fire and ice" or "Italy is the land of culture and food". When we take pupils to a place, we need to do more than reduce it to a set of data to prove a hypothesis or to a narrow, unnuanced headline.

Case study: Dr Paul Ganderton

I am fortunate to be able to look back over a fieldwork-focused career spanning more than four decades and encompassing work in geography, ecology, environmental science, wildlife conservation, geology and archaeology. I look back in wonder and not a bit of sorrow when I contemplate what I used to be able to do and what I can do now. What follows are my thoughts on this situation.

Why do fieldwork?

Quite simply because all these subjects require hands-on experience with objects and situations outside the confines of my classroom. I'll go further: it is not possible to understand these subjects, even in the most elementary way, without field experience. So, for me, fieldwork is not just an integral part of the subject; it's essential and really at the core of subject teaching. Fieldwork connects the pupil and the textbook to what is actually there. It's not as good as the textbook illustrations, it's messy and you need to think about it, but that's the whole point. It is no good talking about research-informed education and cognitive science (both excellent, by the way) and then telling pupils they can't leave their seats. Virtual reality is not fieldwork.

I do it this way because …

Fieldwork is not an adjunct. Given that fieldwork is essential to what I teach, its planning is not an afterthought. Whether I'm planning for a year-long series of lessons in wildlife conservation, a week-long trip to Wales or the Australian Alps, or a quick lesson in the school grounds, everything ties into a sequence to produce better understanding. Fieldwork is a chance to practise what you preach! So, in conservation, we conserve a medieval woodland; in ecology, we use the methods the professionals use to understand invertebrate numbers, and so on. It's never a textbook; it's an authentic experience carrying out investigations using accepted approaches. Fieldwork builds knowledge, understanding and commitment. An enduring memory is of two pupils (hitherto largely disengaged) standing open-mouthed at a glacial valley in Wales. All they could eventually say was that the scene was the same one from the textbook used to introduce the topic two weeks prior. It turned them around. That's why we do fieldwork.

I have found that …

Fieldwork leaves a lasting impression on pupils, and in far more than a subject sense. Working in the field with their peers bonds a group. They actually love doing it. It's different and the memories they make create a bond between them, the subject and the teacher. When the subject is getting tough, just say, "Do you remember when we saw X in that field?" Instant connection with the learning. I have seen and heard field stories passed down from one year to the next. New pupils ask when they are going to do/see X because the last group said they had such a good time. Fieldwork also creates a love for and appreciation of the outdoors. Anything that encourages pupils to care about the environment is a benefit. Fieldwork helps well-being. A pupil's normal habitat is not the classroom (at least it wasn't until recently!). Fieldwork means getting out not just for learning but for a dose of outdoors positivity: it should be the best marketing tool a geography department has.

Finally ...

Fieldwork is under fire universally. Having worked in several systems internationally, all I see now is a move to squeeze fieldwork out of the system. Paperwork and regulations are so time-consuming that most staff (often the less experienced/skilled ones) just don't think it's worth the time, relegating it to as few mandated hours as possible. So much of what made my fieldwork fire light up would not be possible today. So, fight for fieldwork!

Dr Paul Ganderton has worked as a geographer, researcher, writer, teacher and assessor, and is currently a consultant in geography and ecology education and design. He tweets as @ecogeog.

Enquiry approach

Fieldwork is often framed as a form of enquiry:

- Which factors have the greatest impact on the microclimate in our school site?

- How does quality of life change as you move out from the centre of town?

- What impact does coppicing have on processes in the drainage basin?

In each case, the pupils would collect their own data in an effort to answer the question, before analysing what they found and using it to reach a conclusion. However, enquiry in geography does not only belong as part of fieldwork. It is an important part of the discipline and should infuse the way in which we put our curriculum into practice.

Jane Ferretti suggests that enquiry has become a somewhat neglected approach in our classrooms.[8] She suggests that this may be due to a combination of factors, including: the way in which we have been encouraged to structure lessons so that an objective is neatly met within a 60-minute period; the assessment system, which encourages a delivery model of specified content; and the government meddling in the curriculum, which either devalued geographical knowledge (in 2007) or reduced it to a list of content (in 2014). However, she also suggests that we, as teachers, may be to blame, arguing that there is:

> another related issue here too in terms of how teachers see their role: is it simply the transmission of information or should teachers be enabling students to investigate something geographical?[9]

We need to be careful here that we do not set up a false dichotomy between the transfer of information on one hand and geographical enquiry on the other. Enquiry is always built on a foundation of knowledge, and that knowledge has to *come from* somewhere. If pupils are enquiring about the microclimate of their school:

- Their teacher may transmit the knowledge that the south side of the school is hotter.

- Pupils might go to the south side of the school, feel that it is hotter and so have that knowledge transmitted from their environment via experience.

- They might type "why is the south side of the school hotter than the north?" into a search engine and have the information transmitted via a website that they click on.

In all these cases, knowledge – or at least information – has been passed from a source to the pupils, but it is what they do with it that creates enquiry. I think we need to be cautious in assuming that knowledge pupils find by searching online, or experiencing first-hand, is automatically "better" than that shared by their teacher. Indeed, with our expertise in explanation and recontextualising information, I would argue that we should be the primary source of knowledge for our pupils.

8   Jane Ferretti, The enquiry approach in geography. In Mark Jones and David Lambert (eds), *Debates in Geography Education*, 2nd edn (Routledge: Abingdon and New York, 2018), pp. 115–126.
9   Ferretti, The enquiry approach in geography, p. 118.

Margaret Roberts, whose research into the enquiry approach in geography has shaped practice for decades, proposes a framework for enquiry in the classroom that is comprised of four stages:[10]

- Creating a need to know – in which pupils are encouraged to be curious and speculate about an image or set of data. They pose questions, create a hypothesis and look for links to what they already know.

- Using data – in which pupils locate and/or collect the data they will need in order to investigate the topic further. They manipulate this data.

- Making sense – in which pupils analyse this data to reach conclusions.

- Reflecting on learning – in which they consider what they now know and evaluate the process whilst considering weaknesses with their conclusions.

There are many ways to approach such a geographical enquiry at school, but they tend to fall between two poles: pupil-led and teacher-led. In a pupil-led enquiry, the pupils are given more control over the process. They might be involved in identifying anything from the topics they wish to study to the questions to investigate within the topic. They might be given responsibility for deciding what data they need to collect and planning how to achieve this. We see this pupil-led approach to enquiry in the A level NEA, in which the pupil is expected to go through the stages of enquiry with only minimal guidance and support from their teacher. The advantage of this approach is that pupils learn about the enquiry process itself and how disciplinary knowledge is sought in our subject.

However, that this pupil-led approach is found at the very end of their school experience perhaps tells us something of the difficulty of running an enquiry in this way. Trying to bring a true pupil-led approach down the key stages is beset with difficulties.

Firstly, there is the problem of the enquiry being led by pupil interests – and they can only have an interest in that which they already know. This moves us away from our purpose of building powerful knowledge through our curriculum and back towards a preference for the everyday knowledge that pupils bring with them. It also means that you are going to be juggling the competing demands to study topics suggested by each and every pupil, or you will have to select one from those suggested and then, sadly, it is likely that a few loud voices will

---

10 Margaret Roberts, *Learning Through Enquiry: Making Sense of Geography in the Key Stage 3 Classroom* (Sheffield: The Geographical Association, 2003).

dominate. There are also a host of practical problems with the pupil-led approach, such as pupils' ability to gather the kinds of data they may feel they need (due to issues with access, equipment or risk) and the varying timeframes that would be needed to enact the enquiry they propose. Essentially, any curriculum planning you may wish to do becomes impossible and the curriculum becomes purely reactive.

In contrast, the teacher-led approach takes pupils through the enquiry process, but the underpinning decision making has already taken place. The teacher selects the topics, poses the questions and provides the data. They may also give a great deal more guidance to help pupils reach a conclusion based on the data. Whilst this overcomes many of the problems with the pupil-led approach, it does present its own. It is possible that the teacher-led approach will emphasise the learning of the propositional knowledge at the heart of the enquiry (the way in which different factors influence microclimate or the impacts of coppicing) at the expense of wider disciplinary knowledge of how geographers think through an enquiry. We learn by careful, deliberate practice, and this includes the chance to practise things like selecting useful data and forming geographical questions about a topic.

The resolution to this dilemma lies in how we combine teacher- and pupil-led approaches. To keep within the purpose of the curriculum set out in Part I of this book, the department and/or the teacher will need to select the topic. However, we can ensure that we explain to the class why this topic has been chosen and how a geographer would approach its study. There could then be opportunities for pupils to suggest questions and lines of enquiry, as long as they have the necessary prior knowledge to form suitable questions. As is so often the case, what pupils already know shapes what they can do next. The teacher may then curate the information that will be used to answer these questions, but the pupils may be able to reach their own conclusions based on the data provided. Modelling beforehand, and providing feedback afterwards, can ensure that the conclusions reached are plausible and well justified.

An enquiring curriculum in practice

There are a number of steps we can take to ensure that a culture of enquiry is embedded in our curriculum.

Step 1: frame through a question

When you look at your curriculum, ask yourself what question you are seeking to answer about a particular topic. What *quests for truth* are your pupils on? You can use this to help create a fertile question that will sit at the heart of the topic. Answering this question becomes your enquiry.

Yoram Harpaz suggests that a fertile question should have six characteristics.[11] The table that follows gives an explanation of these characteristics along with an example of how they might apply to a topic on microclimate.

Characteristics of fertile questions	Example
An open question – there should be more than one possible answer to the question.	"How does the school's microclimate influence the way in which people use the site?" is a better fertile question than "Which side of the school has the highest temperature?"
An undermining question – misconceptions should be challenged.	There may be a misconception that areas exposed to the sun are always going to be the hottest, ignoring other factors like the influence of buildings and surface colour.

---

11 Yoram Harpaz, Teaching and learning in a community of thinking, *Journal of Curriculum and Supervision* 20(2) (2005): 136–157.

Characteristics of fertile questions	Example
	We might therefore want to ask, "Why do people avoid the quad in the summer?"
A rich question – it should be based on powerful knowledge that needs to be researched and thought about.	We don't want the answer to be immediately obvious and pupils should need to work hard to reach a strong conclusion. Therefore, "How will the microclimate of our school be different over the course of the year?" could be a good question that encourages the application of theory by making predictions.
A connected question – there should be links to different parts of the discipline as well as the potential to connect to their everyday knowledge.	If we are going to connect to different topics, we might ask, "How could we change our school site to adapt to the impacts of climate change?"
A charged question – ethical dimensions of the question should be explored.	We could adapt the previous question to add an ethical slant by framing it as "Should we change our school site to adapt to the impacts of climate change?" as this would allow for consideration of whether mitigation or adaptation is the more responsible solution.
A practical question – it needs to be within the ability of pupils to get hold of the information they need to answer the question.	This can often be a barrier to A level pupils' NEA enquiries. In this instance, we would want to be wary of questions like "How has the school's microclimate changed over

Characteristics of fertile questions	Example
	the last century?" unless you have the data to give them.

Step 2: source the information

Whatever your enquiry, your pupils are going to need information with which to enquire. This might come in the form of charts, teacher explanations, raw data, graphs, maps, photographs, case studies, interviews, diagrams, articles, videos, educational materials in the form of textbooks or worksheets ... the list is endless. Whatever the type of information, you will need to decide where to source it from, and this involves the difficult task of resource curation. Geography educator David Rayner calls on teachers to be the "resourceful teacher" who:

> is able to understand the pros and cons of resource selection and is able to select, create and bring together exciting and relevant student resources that engage and promote geographical learning.[12]

He also states the importance of being a "resource critic" who evaluates the usefulness of the information they select and create.

Here are a few questions to consider when collating resources for pupils:

- Do they have the foundational knowledge necessary to make sense of the information? There is little point in providing a compound line graph showing the changing energy mix in the UK if they either do not know how to read this type of graph or do not know what the types of energy are.

- Is the information up to date? Situations in geography are shifting constantly. Neighbourhood-level data on inequality may shift year on year (which in itself would be an interesting line of enquiry) and the resources need to be regularly checked and updated.

12 David Rayner, Resources. In Mark Jones (ed.), *The Handbook of Secondary Geography* (Sheffield: The Geographical Association, 2017), pp. 150–165 at p. 164.

- Whose story are we telling? It can be very easy to find ourselves providing detailed evidence to support the conclusion that we want to lead our class to and providing cursory, at best, information on counterpoints. Geography is usually more complex and the resources we use in an enquiry should reflect that. If there is one absolute right answer, perhaps an enquiry approach is the wrong one.

- How authentic is the resource? In needing to simplify complex ideas we might mock-up a resource: a simple set of data or a fake news article. However, where possible we want to introduce our pupils to the real world, and we run the risk of obscuring this behind ersatz materials.

- Whose voice are we hearing? Related to the question of authenticity is the question of which people are represented in our resources. If we are conducting an enquiry about Haiti, do we hear from people who live there, and do we hear from a wide range of people? It can be very easy to rely on video clips from aid agencies or news reporters that miss the stories of the people who can best represent the place.

Step 3: create the need to know

Once you know the question you want your pupils to be able to answer, you can start thinking about why they might want to answer it. Of course, we can always fall back on "because I told them to", and that might get us so far, but by creating an intrinsic motivation to find the answer we are more likely to encourage them to think hard about the question and form links to other topics as they puzzle it out. This process is largely invisible to us, so it is hard to police and therefore to insist upon. If pupils only ever answer questions "because they have to", we run the risk that they will comply by getting the work done but with minimal thinking: not enough to create meaningful learning.

So how do we create the intrinsic motivation to enquire? Creating a fertile question should help as it will mean that the question will be intriguing. It is this intrigue that we want to build upon. We can do this by presenting our fertile enquiry question alongside images that help to illustrate the mystery at hand. For example, to launch an enquiry into the question "Why is Haiti the poorest country in the western hemisphere?" we could use a picture that contrasts Haiti with its neighbour, the Dominican Republic: one that shows the stark border between the two countries marked by lush forest on one side and bare, deforested hills on the other. Humans are naturally curious and we do not like questions going unanswered. It should not take much to frame an enquiry in such a way that this curiosity is triggered and the enquiry turned into a need to know.

Step 4: using data

In this step our pupils begin to collect the information they will need in order to answer the enquiry question. The terms "information" and "data" are used here in their widest possible sense: we want them to find out anything they did not already know about the topic along with calling on relevant prior learning. Looking through and making sense of this data is likely to take several lessons as fertile enquiry questions are by their nature rich and complex. It is also likely that pupils will work on smaller sources of information one by one and slowly build them up into something larger. It would be a mistake to simply hand over a folder of information and ask them to use it to answer the enquiry question.

For example, we might have as our enquiry question: "To what extent are portrayals of East Africa out of date?" This could involve:

- Pupils considering their everyday knowledge of East Africa and where this knowledge comes from.

- They could then be introduced to portrayals of the region (such as maps and stories from the media) that they may not have come across before. They could put this together to answer the question "How has East Africa been portrayed in the past?"

- A range of maps showing cartographic data on climate, biomes and population densities so that they can answer questions about the diversity of landscapes.

- Looking at contemporary images of the region today to show the diversity of experience.

- Exploring development indicators for countries across the region and contrasting what the data suggests with the images they have seen.

- Reading written accounts of life in East Africa along with news articles about economic development and the barriers people still face.

All of this would be done over a number of lessons and supported through careful explanation from the teacher, who will help their pupils make sense of the information they are receiving.

Step 5: reaching a conclusion

Once the class have had the time to thoroughly explore a range of information that relates to their question, they should be in a position to answer it. At this point, we want to make sure that they can answer the question *geographically* and show that they are thinking like geographers. This might involve referring to geographical models to see whether they work in this context or discussing them in light of other geographical theories. This is also the point at which we might want to start showing how this question could link to and build on prior learning. For example, with our East Africa question, we could ask them to draw on previous lessons looking at emerging economies or urbanisation.

One thing that will be important in this step of the enquiry is modelling and scaffolding how we want the answer to be written. Fertile enquiry questions are by their nature complex and controversial and there is always a risk that their answers will fail to reflect this. We will probably need to break the question up into sub-questions and explain to pupils how and why we are doing this. For example:

"To what extent are portrayals of East Africa out of date?"

- Explore the question – what do we mean by a "portrayal" in geography? Consider formal and informal representations of place.

- Location of the region – it is always important in geography that we establish the place and its boundaries.

- How was the region portrayed? In order to say to what extent it is out of date, we need to give examples. Discussing each one will give us our structure:

  > Poor – evidence it was portrayed in this way and evidence that the portrayal is out of date.

> ⟩   Rural – as above.

> ⟩   Savanna landscape – as above.

◉   Conclusion – what have you learnt? Discussion of "to what extent".

By going through this process we aren't just modelling how we want pupils to approach this question; we are modelling how a geographer would approach this *type* of question.

Step 6: evaluate the process

This final step is one that often seems to be missed in the rush to move from topic to topic but it is central to helping pupils develop powerful disciplinary knowledge. One of the key differences between a Future 1 and a Future 3 approach to knowledge is that in Future 3 the knowledge is seen as contestable; we are aware that geography is always being created and challenged as our understanding shifts. In this sixth enquiry step we need to help our pupils to evaluate the answer they have reached. We can do this by posing a series of questions about their work. For example:

◉   Did everyone reach the same conclusion? If not, why not?

◉   What evidence might someone else have used that you did not?

◉   How reliable was the information you used?

◉   How valid was the information you used?

◉   Is your conclusion true just at this moment in time? Might it change in the future?

◉   What are the implications of your conclusion? What actions might it suggest should be taken?

These are very complex questions. You might not use them all with every enquiry but they should be planned in throughout the curriculum so that pupils have the opportunities to develop a critical perspective on disciplinary knowledge.

Case study: Catherine Owen

Good enquiry learning is not just leaving pupils to find out an answer for themselves; it is a carefully considered and planned approach to teaching. David Leat discusses how the idea of enquiry, in which we engage every day, is a process of learning worthy of consideration, without rejecting the best of traditional schooling.[13] He refers to Sfard's[14] suggestion that there are two metaphors for learning:

- Acquisition – how facts and pieces of knowledge are "received, acquired, constructed, internalised, appropriated, transmitted, attained, developed, accumulated or grasped."

- Participation – "learning through doing in a particular context".[15]

Enquiry learning requires teachers to consider both of these metaphors. They must be clear about what their pupils will learn and how they will learn it in the appropriate context.

"Learning through doing" could involve pupils heading off to do their own research, but there is a danger of them vanishing down rabbit holes, getting lost or potentially coming across something inappropriate if using the internet. Good enquiry learning needs to be planned carefully to ensure that pupils make good use of their time and find the process beneficial. The "doing" could be something as simple as reading and critiquing an article or applying learning from earlier in the lesson in a decision-making exercise. Acquisition could be likened to Rosenshine's presentation of material in small steps, asking questions and providing models, whilst participation could be likened to practice (first guided, then independent).[16]

---

13 David Leat (ed.), *Enquiry and Project Based Learning: Students, School and Society* (Abingdon and New York: Routledge, 2017).
14 Anna Sfard, On two metaphors for learning and the dangers of choosing just one, *Educational Researcher* 27(2) (1998): 4–13.
15 Leat, *Enquiry and Project Based Learning*, p. 3.
16 Rosenshine, Principles of instruction.

Leat describes curriculum as:

> an expression of our vision of future society, not just a document about what pupils are taught in schools.[17]

This is likely to chime with geography teachers, as our subject is so much more than learning facts and supports pupils in developing their view of the world:

> The experience of school can have profound effects on how people see themselves, how they conduct their lives, how they see and interact with others who are different from themselves, how they conceive of the world and therefore how they see their role and responsibility in wider society.[18]

Our vision for geography at The King Alfred School and Academy focuses on connection – we want our pupils to be connected:

- To success through high attainment and aspiration.
- To contemporary issues shaping the world around us.
- To our local community.
- To the wider world.
- Through technology.
- Through partnerships and teacher development.

Enquiry learning enables us to enact this vision. We use enquiry learning flexibly and in a range of ways in our curriculum. For a while we used enquiry questions as the titles of every topic, but we've since changed this to use shorter, snappy titles where it seemed appropriate. An example is that we used to have a topic called "How do plants and animals adapt to extreme environments?" which we now simply call "extreme environments" – the question still runs through the topic and we discuss it regularly with the pupils, but we use

17 Leat, *Enquiry and Project Based Learning*, p. 3.
18 Leat, *Enquiry and Project Based Learning*, p. 3.

the short title to link together resources for the topic, and so on. There is no need to be chained to a particular way of doing things; your approach needs to fit your pupils and department.

Most of our enquiries take place in the context of the classroom, sometimes making use of technology for research. An example is a lesson asking, "What is the danger of the single story?" In the acquisition phase, the teacher explains what a single story is, illustrating this with Chimamanda Ngozi Adichie's TED Talk.[19] Questioning is used to check understanding and the dangers of stereotypes and misconceptions discussed. The participation phase starts by looking at photographs showing poverty in Uganda, projected on the board, with pupils writing a description of the single story being portrayed. A much wider range of photographs of Uganda is then shared and pupils describe the richer, more complex story. Pupils are given the freedom to research a low-income country of their choice using tablet computers, starting by searching for the country on the BBC News website to see if there is a single story presented and then using a series of recommended websites to explore the country's culture, landscape, tourism and more. They are also challenged to think about whether single stories are also told about high-income countries, whether this is as much of a danger as it is for low-income countries, and whether labelling a place a low-income country is damaging.

One of the wonderful things about geography teaching is the range of contexts we find ourselves in, with fieldwork opening the world to us. Pupils can benefit greatly from following a more formal enquiry process for fieldwork:

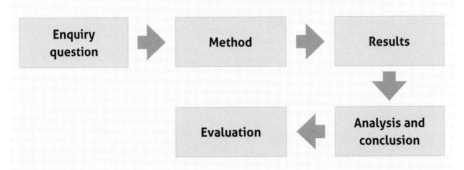

19 Chimamanda Ngozi Adichie, The danger of a single story [video], *TedGlobal* (July 2009). Available at: https://www.ted.com/talks/chimamanda_ngozi_adichie_the_danger_of_a_single_story.

Following this method from their very first fieldwork enquiry will develop their investigation skills, helping them when they answer GCSE exam questions about fieldwork and undertake their A level NEA, but also providing a framework which they will be able to use beyond education. We carry out fieldwork in the school grounds and further afield. An example of an enquiry question is "How sustainable is the Temple Quarter regeneration scheme?" Our Year 10 pupils learn about the Egan Wheel in lessons and choose elements of it to investigate on a field visit to Bristol, using a robust enquiry process to apply geographical theory to a real place.[20]

Well-designed enquiries also maximise the opportunities for interleaving, linking the current enquiry back to elements of previous work. Over time pupils will build their core, propositional and procedural knowledge. Careful planning at the lesson, topic and phase level is key.

Catherine Owen is head of geography at The King Alfred School and Academy and an SLE for The Priory Learning Trust. She tweets as @GeogMum.

Geographic information systems

Geographic information systems (GIS) are tools that allow for both the visualisation and spatial analysis of geographical information.[21] Perhaps the most widely used GIS tools in schools are provided by Esri ArcGIS.[22] Such software allows for the display of a huge array of data sets to be laid over the earth's surface and allows for the identification of correlations between different distributions. The possibilities are almost endless but could involve anything from looking at the amount of storm damage depending on the height of the land to crime statistics across areas with different levels of deprivation. GIS software can also allow pupils

20 John Egan, *The Egan Review: Skills for Sustainable Communities* (London: Office of the Deputy Prime Minister, 2004). Available at: https://www.ihbc.org.uk/recent_papers/docs/Egan%20Review%20Skills%20for%20sustainable%20Communities.pdf.

21 Mary Fargher, GIS and other geospatial technologies. In Mark Jones (ed.), *The Handbook of Secondary Geography* (Sheffield: The Geographical Association, 2017), pp. 244–259.

22 See https://www.esri.com/en-us/arcgis/about-arcgis/overview.

to collect their own precisely geo-located data and upload the data set for analysis.

Its use has been mandated in the national curriculum since 2007, but uptake in schools has been patchy at best, with Ofsted reporting that only a small number of schools are using it effectively.[23] One of the biggest barriers to its wider use in schools is that the software is not especially intuitive. Geography teachers may be offered a day's training on it during their ITT but if they do not have subsequent opportunities to practise with it, their confidence will not develop. There has also perhaps been an issue with the assumption that pupils should be in front of the computer using the software themselves. This presents challenges in terms of finding the time to teach them how to use the complex technology effectively, as well as having access to computer rooms for the block of time required to do this well. However, GIS can be used effectively by the teacher at the front of the classroom, as discussed here by Alistair Hamill.

Case study: Alistair Hamill

When I first started teaching in the 1990s, to get access to up-to-date geographical information I had to buy these old-fashioned things called newspapers. I would find the article I was interested in, carefully cut it out, and give it pride of place on the "Geography in the news" noticeboard, watching it slowly yellow over the months and years that followed.

Today, however, in our internet and open source world, we have easier access than ever to an unprecedented amount of data. So much so that the challenge is no longer access but managing the sheer volume of data no further than a mouse click away. More than ever we need powerful data presentation and visualisation tools to allow us to manipulate the data sets, to enable us to search for patterns, correlations and anomalies.

---

23 Mary Fargher, Using Geographic Information (GI). In Mark Jones and David Lambert (eds), *Debates in Geography Education*, 2nd edn (Abingdon and New York: Routledge, 2018), pp. 197–223.

Luckily, geography has its very own bespoke software to help us do just that: GIS. Like any data software, it crunches the numbers in vast data sets easily and readily. But its magic lies in its ability to spatialise that data – to turn maps from static data visualisations into interactive and highly powerful data analysis tools in a way hitherto not possible.

In my classes, this allows me to unlock some powerful geography with my pupils. One exercise we do involves looking at the impacts of Typhoon Haiyan, with a focus on scale and pattern. Having started with a global overview of where tropical storms occur, we can zoom in to look at the Philippines as a whole, turning on a layer of the storm track and another of a choropleth map of damage.

But we can zoom in further, looking at proportional circles showing storm surge height on one of the islands. In most cases, as distance from the storm track increases, storm surge height decreases. But the proportional circles reveal some anomalies. We can use the measure tool to find out just how far away they are. Then we can manipulate the scale once again. If this were a static map from a yellowing newspaper clipping, we would be left scratching our heads, wondering what might cause those anomalies. But this is a GIS map, and we can zoom in to explore further. We can get down to the very local scale, where we discover that the topography reveals a bay. We can speculate how a bay might influence the storm surge as it approaches, how it might funnel it in, causing the wave to rise. We can go in ever further. We can look street by street in Tacloban City. We can turn on a layer of building damage, using the measuring tool to calculate the area of buildings destroyed vs damaged.

The first time I used this with a sixth form class, I realised it can unleash even more depth of understanding. "Mr Hamill," said one of my pupils, "I'm just wondering here, is there a relationship between building size and whether or not they were destroyed?" I hadn't even noticed this when preparing the task, but giving pupils the ability to control scale and features like this prompted them to apply their knowledge and spot patterns for themselves. Now our interest was piqued, we zoomed in further, even going as far as to virtually stand in the street, looking all around at the individual buildings, seeing how the shanty towns were particularly vulnerable due to their location by the sea and flimsy manner of construction. From the global pattern, to the street view, with all sorts of scales in-between. This indeed is a very effective tool to turn space into place.

I call this approach "scaffolded freedom". We cover the content about Typhoon Haiyan before, so this is not a free-for-all. We carefully build the requisite knowledge beforehand. But GIS allows pupils to apply their knowledge in a powerful way that guides them to discover how the theory applies in the real world, and enables them to conduct their own journeys of discovery too.

I still look back with fondness at the yellowing newspaper clippings that adorned my walls, but I would never go back to them if it meant losing the most powerful of data visualisation and manipulation tool that is GIS.

Alistair Hamill is an experienced geography teacher, a head of geography and a textbook author. He tweets as @lcgeography.

Questions

- What role does fieldwork currently play in your geography curriculum and how do you ensure that it leads to learning?

- Can you see the potential for teacher-led enquiry in the curriculum? How big a role, do you think, do pupil decisions need to play in the enquiry process?

- What barriers do you see to the effective use of GIS in your curriculum? How could they be overcome?

Further reading

John Widdowson and Alan Parkinson, *Fieldwork Through Enquiry* (Sheffield: The Geographical Association, 2013).

Margaret Roberts, *Geography Through Enquiry: Approaches to Teaching and Learning in the Secondary School* (Sheffield: The Geographical Association, 2013).

Chapter 10

Geography for the 21st century

If geography is "writing the world", then one problem we face when creating the curriculum is the fast pace of change we see around us. This may suggest either that the purpose of the curriculum needs to be in constant flux or that our schemes of work – the practical implementation of the curriculum – need to be constantly rewritten. This chapter considers the extent to which we should attempt to align our curriculum with changing purposes and changing content.

Responding to drivers of change

As geographers we are probably more aware than anyone of the fast pace of change in the world. Even at GCSE level we expect our pupils to understand how technological, demographic and environmental changes in a society lead to different impacts and responses. To what extent should the purpose and practice of our curriculum reflect these drivers of change? Should we teach in a different way to reflect increased automation from technology or shifts in the job market brought around by demographic changes? Should the purpose of our curriculum reflect the climate emergency? There are certainly those who suggest it should.

Stephen Heppell argues that technological changes should lead to a revolution in our schools. We need to move away from schools that are designed to produce factory workers. He says:

> The industrial model of education served us well for many, many decades. Doors shut, bells ringing, everyone eating at the same time. We had factories like that once, too.[1]

His argument is that new technology renders such schools obsolete both because there are new ways in which pupils can learn, with increased independence, accessing information from technology rather than their teacher, and because schools prepare pupils for work in factories that no longer exist. It would certainly be possible to design a geography curriculum around the purpose of responding to technological change. We could set pupils up with a minimally guided enquiry task and then simply step back and facilitate them as they work in groups to try to address it. However, just because we *can* does not mean that we *should*. The teacher is almost certainly the greatest resource in the classroom when it comes to not only subject knowledge but the knowledge of how to make it accessible to their pupils. By taking a back seat we leave pupils – who are, let's not forget, novices in the subject, who lack the detailed disciplinary knowledge that we have – to make meaning as best they can from the information they find for themselves online. We risk leaving them overwhelmed and falling back on simplistic conclusions. If we want our pupils to become independent learners who are able to take advantage of the vast quantities of information that technology gives them access to, we need to equip them with the solid disciplinary foundations that will allow them to make sense of it. This is the end point of our purpose and should not be mistaken for the method of achieving it.

Another misconception in Heppell's argument is that schools, as they are currently set up, are creating workers for factories. However, as any geographer could tell him, it has now been a number of generations since factories provided the bulk of employment opportunities of most areas of the UK. This change in employment structure has been shifting slowly since the second half of the 20th century and yet during this time a traditional approach to the structure of schools (desks in

1   Stephen Heppell, Schools of the future must adjust to technological needs, *The Sydney Morning Herald* (16 February 2015). Available at: https://www.smh.com.au/opinion/schools-of-the-future-must-adjust-to-technology-needs-20150216-13fpj9.html.

rows, teacher instruction, etc.) hasn't stopped the UK in leading the way with the rise of creative industries and the knowledge economy. Creativity is based on strong foundations of powerful knowledge. Indeed, the starting premise of this argument, that our schools were ever set up to provide factories with workers, seems fundamentally flawed. If this were the case it seems unlikely that we would bother teaching them any curriculum content at all. We would have created schools more in the form of a Future 2 curriculum with its emphasis on useful employable skills than Future 1's lists of facts to be recalled.

New technology inevitably brings changes to our classrooms because it gives us access to new pedagogical tools. We can use GIS and virtual reality (VR) to bring places to life and put high-quality geographical data in everyone's hands. But this technology does not lead to change in the purpose that we outlined in Part I or in the practice outlined here in Part II.

The arguments of those who propose repurposing education around issues of environmental sustainability take a similar form. Paul Warwick makes the case for Education for Sustainable Development (ESD) by stating that:

> Children and young people are growing up in the midst of multiple points of planetary crisis including climate change, extreme poverty, biodiversity loss, widening socio-economic inequality, and the weakening of oceanic and terrestrial ecosystems (UNESCO, 2015).[2]

I suspect that there will be few geography teachers who do not recognise the crisis the planet is facing and the importance of teaching pupils to be knowledgeable about such matters. However, Warwick goes much further in arguing that this should change the purpose and practice of education. He states that:

> Education for Sustainable Development represents a global education reform movement that has as its fundamental aim learners developing the competencies required to contribute towards social justice and environmental stewardship goals.[3]

---

2   Paul Warwick, Education for Sustainable Development: a movement towards pedagogies of civic compassion, *Forum* 58(3) (2016): 407–414 at 407.
3   Warwick, Education for Sustainable Development, 412.

This aim is achieved through a Future Leaders Programme which:

> has drawn in particular from participatory models of how students can actively shape their own learning, such as Hart's (1997) ladder of children's participation and more recently Fielding's (2011) patterns of partnership typology.[4]

What we see with ESD is a return to a Future 2 curriculum model that promotes generic qualities like compassion above pupils' capability to do and be as they see fit based on what they have learnt. It is notable that both Heppell's call for educational reform to reflect technological and demographic drivers of change and Warwick's call for reform to combat environmental crises both start with arguments about curriculum and purpose but end with very similar calls for pedagogical changes. These are the same types of changes (teachers as facilitators, a pupil-led curriculum, etc.) that progressive educators have called for over the last few decades, irrespective of the drivers for change to which they claim to be responding.[5] This approach also seems to bring us back to the geography of good intentions warned of by Marsden and Standish (discussed in Chapter 4) that risks removing the very thing, the powerful geographical knowledge, that would best enable pupils to respond to planetary crises in the future. It is here – in the content of *what* we teach, rather than in the purpose of *why* we teach – that the geography classroom needs to constantly evolve.

Curriculum content and the changing world

Perhaps more so than in any other subject, geographical knowledge is always changing: county borders shift, heads of state come and go, governmental policies change, our knowledge about physical processes – such as those leading to earthquakes – evolves, and so on. When I started teaching in the early noughties, it was common to teach the tiger economies of South-East Asia as "newly industrialised countries". Now, not only has the term been replaced with "newly emerging economies" but most of those countries have moved beyond that categorisation of

---

4   Warwick, Education for Sustainable Development, 410.
5   Robert Peal, *Progressively Worse: The Burden of Bad Ideas in British Schools* (London: Civitas, 2014).

development. Likewise, the teaching of informal settlements has shifted from the cities of Brazil to India and now, in many cases, to areas like Kibera in Nairobi, Kenya. We taught convection currents in the mantle as the main driving force of plate movement rather than ridge-push and slab-pull. In just a couple of decades the number of such changes are immeasurable, and starting to list them makes me feel very old.

Sometimes the replacement of old ideas with new ones seems straightforward but at other points this is beset by complexities and debates. One such debate was played out in the pages of the Geographical Association's journal, *Teaching Geography*, and concerned the teaching of the Burgess model. This model attempts to explain how cities develop in similar ways, with different land uses falling into broadly concentric circles moving out from a central business district. Charles Rawding argues that:

> The wholesale adoption of the Burgess model has fossilised our understanding of the incredibly dynamic nature of urban landscapes; more seriously, it renders sterile the urban landscapes we introduce to our students.[6]

The Burgess model was developed in Chicago in the 1920s, based on observations of that city, and its wholescale application to cities around the world is both out of date and out of place. Rawding argues that it should no longer be used in our schools.

So far, so straightforward. Out-of-date geographical models should be consigned to the bin. However, in a response in the next volume Steve Puttick states that there is still a place for the Burgess model in our classrooms. His argument is that:

> I want to suggest that the challenge for geography education is to better understand the context of knowledge production and to critically engage with representation. To put it another way, I believe that how teachers use models is more important than the models themselves.[7]

6 Charles Rawding, Raising issues: putting Burgess in the bin, *Teaching Geography* 44(3) (2019): 94–96 at 94.
7 Steve Puttick, Raising issues: taking Burgess out of the bin, *Teaching Geography* 45(1) (2020): 6–8 at 6.

Puttick views an understanding of the Burgess model as useful in school geography, as it enables pupils to see the influence the model had and the ways in which geographers use and contest models.

We can see here a microcosm of the wider debate about the role of knowledge in the classroom. Puttick's claim is that the problem is with the way in which the model is taught in schools as a geographical fact (Future 1) rather than as a contested idea (Future 3). This would suggest that when updating schemes of work, we want to keep one eye on what is removed so that we can discuss the reason for its removal alongside the new material. In this way our ever-evolving curriculum has disciplinary thinking built into the process.

At other times we may want to change our curriculum in light of new developments in our subject. This can be done in a deep or surface way. An example of a surface change would be to include topics that relate to immediate concerns and interests in the media. For example, following the broadcast of *Blue Planet II* – and the spotlight it shone on the impacts of plastics on marine ecosystems – there was a proliferation of schemes of work being written about the issue and dropped into existing programmes of study. The advantage of this approach is that it can, when done well, illustrate the role that geography plays in understanding these complex problems. Pupils could learn about plastic as a resource management issue that considers both why it is so commonly used and the problems of disposal and its lasting legacy. Here we might pose a fertile question like: "Do the environmental benefits of single-use plastics outweigh the disadvantages?" This would allow pupils to look at the issue in a depth that surpasses the everyday knowledge presented by the media.

However, there are disadvantages to building or reforming your curriculum in such a way. Firstly, adding something into your programme of study is going to displace something else. If your curriculum has been planned with purpose, then that previous unit was included for a reason and is in that place in the sequence because it will be built on in the future. Removing it means that the knowledge that subsequent topics will rely on is not there. For example, you might replace a Year 7 sustainable energy topic with one looking at plastic, but this could then mean having to adapt the Year 8 topic on Russia which is predicated on pupils knowing something about fossil fuel use.

Another potential problem is that this approach leads to us teaching geography as though the purpose is to make pupils believe a certain thing or behave in a certain way. The unit on plastics becomes nothing more than "Why is the use of plastic a bad thing?" which is not in itself a particularly geographical question, as we can see if we view it through the lens of Jackson's geographical big ideas (see page 58).

This kind of question can result in the topic being relatively detached from a sense of place, or places being seen simply as either the victim or perpetrator of the problem. There may be some sense of personal connection ("My use of plastics does X elsewhere") but it is unlikely to go much further. This kind of simplistic single story leads us back to Marsden's warning regarding the geography of good intentions that take the geography out of geography education. However, unpicking this can give us some indicators of how the topic could be approached in a more geographical way.

For example, we could start by ensuring that the issue of single-use plastics is rooted in a study of a real place that has been impacted. We could pick some far-flung destination where plastic is sent for recycling and discuss the problems with this: poor working conditions, unsanitary conditions, etc. However, this would risk presenting a very simplistic view of place and of relationships between countries. A solution could be to pick a place where plastics are sent that your curriculum already covers in some depth and look at the issue in the context of what pupils already know about that country. Your pupils may already know a great deal about China and its race for economic development, so looking at the plastic that arrives there for recycling becomes more nuanced and interesting. Their prior knowledge on China's development and move towards a consumerist culture can also raise the question of where *their* plastic waste goes, the changing flows of waste and resources around the world, and links to development. Now we are also considering issues of scale and connection.

This also begins to touch on Jackson's concept of relational thinking and the power relationships at play. Who is making the decisions and who is dealing with the fallout? What agency do the different players have to effect change? We might build in thinking about proximity and distance with plastic waste by considering where it falls in people's priorities. Is it seen as a distant problem – far removed from the actions of the individual person – and, therefore, are we less likely to see action to tackle it than with a more immediate concern? When action is taken, is it the *right* action that will lead to the biggest impact or simply the most visible?

What pupils learn through being taught about this issue in light of geography's big ideas can then be applied to a more complex and less leading question. Instead of

"Why is the use of plastic a bad thing?" we might ask something like "How does China's rapid economic development affect the global flow of plastic?" Doing this brings the geography back in.

We may also want to review our curriculum in a deeper way than simply adding new topics to address contemporary issues. We do this to reflect bigger changes within our discipline that may influence teaching across our curriculum. One example of this would be the increasing awareness that geography's heritage is one of colonialism and empire, the legacy of which continues to this day. The Black Lives Matter protests of 2020 have led to a great deal of soul searching in many academic disciplines, geography included, and to the realisation that the voices of people of colour have often been under-represented and their experiences ignored in favour of a white, western perspective of their geographies. This could influence our teaching of a number of different topics but is likely to be most immediately relevant when teaching development studies, which has long been accused of paternalism. It would also be relevant when looking at challenges in urban areas, such as the growth of informal settlements, to ensure that the voices of the inhabitants are represented and the situation is not viewed only through the lens of our own priorities and concerns. There are also interesting intersections with environmental concerns, specifically regarding differing views on how these should best be approached – for example, the concerns of some indigenous groups about the REDD+ scheme to tackle deforestation and the implications for land ownership.

Another example of a more radical reform to our curriculum comes from our growing understanding of the Anthropocene. The term "Anthropocene" has been proposed as the title for the geological epoch that we now find ourselves in, following on from the post-glacial Holocene epoch. "Anthro-" points to this being the *human* epoch, suggested as there is now significant evidence that the impact which humans are having on the world will transcend our immediate environment and have a lasting impact in the geological record. The exact start of this epoch is hotly debated, with suggestions ranging from the start of settled farming – when large numbers of domesticated animal bones begin to appear in fossil records – to the industrial revolution of the late 19th century, with its increased carbon emissions, or even the mid-20th century and the advent of nuclear testing.

What the concept of the Anthropocene does is challenge our ideas about the extent to which human actions impact on the whole world and encourages us to embrace geography's holistic nature. Once again, we need to move beyond the silo model discussed in Chapter 8. As Charles Rawding explains:

> Holistic approaches to geography are essential if, as geographers, we are to achieve our stated aim of understanding the Earth in all its complexity and they underpin any understanding of the subdivisions within the subject.[8]

Rawding gives an example of teaching about *neobiota* (species that have spread beyond their original territory because of human intervention) through the example of wild fig trees growing in Yorkshire, the seeds of which have been spread via the sewage works with the conditions for growth provided by the river water warmed by the cooling plant of the local power station.[9]

The Anthropocene is a powerful concept which brings together the disparate sub-domains of geography, encouraging us to think geographically and see the world in new ways. It could influence our teaching of ecosystems by acknowledging the problematic idea of "natural" during this epoch. When teaching aspects of geology and the rock cycle, we will need to address the appearance of microplastics in new sedimentary rock. There are few areas of geography that will be unaffected by this concept.

Creating a garden of peace

A powerful curriculum is a living thing that will shift and evolve over time. This is inevitable because powerful knowledge is created and contested in academic disciplines and it is this powerful knowledge that we seek to teach. However, I would suggest that we should think very carefully when changing our curriculum to ensure that we are altering it in light of our purpose. It is all too easy for the original aims of a curriculum to become lost when things are added and removed as fashions and interests come and go. Before we know it, the coherence that we

8 Charles Rawding, Challenging assumptions: the importance of holistic geographies, *Geography* 98(3) (2013): 157–159 at 157.
9 Charles Rawding, The Anthropocene and the global. In Mark Jones and David Lambert (eds), *Debates in Geography Education*, 2nd edn (Abingdon and New York: Routledge, 2018), pp. 240–249.

worked so hard to achieve is lost, we are back to a seemingly random collection of topics, and the geography is buried behind the good intentions.

When thinking about the competing demands on our curriculum I am reminded once again of David Wadley's idea of gardens of peace.[10] His argument was that academic institutions need to be gardens of peace in which scholars can contemplate and reach conclusions in their own *quests for truth*. These gardens of peace need to be removed from the clamour and bright lights of the neoliberal city that would like scholars to serve its needs instead. There will be those who will call for the issue of the moment to be included in our curriculum, who will suggest – against all evidence to the contrary – that it would be solved if only schools would teach it, but we need to stand fast to our purpose and tend our own gardens. This is why I have argued throughout this book that we must begin with a very clear idea of the purpose of schools, of geography and of our own curriculum, and of the principles behind this purpose. These ideas act as our constant guides when contemplating what we teach and to what end.

10 Wadley, The garden of peace.

Conclusion

Alongside my day job, I have been writing and talking about education since 2015, which means that teachers sometimes tell me that things I have written and said have been used in their CPD sessions. Members of their senior leadership team (SLT) might use something from a book or article or share an idea from a conference, webinar or Twitter. That is, of course, lovely. I only write in the hope of being read and because I believe in what I am writing. However, as an experienced teacher it also fills me with a certain amount of dread as I have seen what can happen to good ideas as they are passed on from person to person; they mutate into something new.

We see this mutation all the time in education:[1]

- The principle of dual coding (organising information in such a way that visual prompts support what is being said) becomes adding icons to PowerPoint slides.

- The need to get pupils answering questions without relying on them putting their hands up leads to teachers clutching pots of numbered lollypop sticks.

- An acknowledgement of the power of feedback in the classroom results in triple marking in different coloured pens.

Over the last decade we have seen a knowledge turn in our schools, meaning we have moved away from a Future 2 conception of knowledge in the curriculum and towards what could either be a Future 1 or Future 3 position. Many schools, through published curriculum intent statements, are certainly using the language of Future 3, with their commitments to powerful knowledge, equitable access, social justice and strong disciplines, but it would be all too easy for this to mutate into a far simpler Future 1 model. Indeed, we may be seeing this happen already. Signs of such a mutation might include:

- Attempting to pin down a list of what every pupil needs to remember as some form of knowledge organiser that pupils are then expected to learn.

---

1 Enser, Education myths: an origin story.

- Using retrieval practice to recall facts and figures without ever giving the pupils the opportunity to *do* something with this information.

- A curriculum that talks about disciplinary knowledge but only focuses on the outcomes of this knowledge and not the ways in which it was created.

This is not to say that knowledge organisers, quizzes or a focus on propositional knowledge is a bad thing, but they do not in and of themselves lead to powerful knowledge. If we are going to create a powerful geography curriculum then we need to ensure that we are not distracted by the surface details (the pedagogical tools) until we have the underpinning curriculum purpose in place. We can do this by working through the following steps.

Step 1: purpose

Spend some time as a department considering your own views on the purpose of geography education to see if there is any kind of alignment. You could do this by considering which of the ideological traditions proposed by Eleanor Rawling – and shown in the table that follows – you most closely ascribe to.[2]

Ideological tradition	The purpose of geography is to ...
Utilitarianism	Get a suitable job and live a good life. The focus should therefore be on teaching information that has a purpose in life after school.
Cultural restorationism	Pass on an agreed (and largely unchanging) body of knowledge and skills that would otherwise be lost to the next generation.
Liberal humanist	Pass on the cultural heritage from generation to generation through geographical big ideas and intellectual challenge.

2   Eleanor Rawling, Ideology, politics and curriculum change: reflections on school geography 2000, *Geography* 85(3) (2000): 209–220.

Ideological tradition	The purpose of geography is to ...
Progressive educational	Develop the whole child by developing general competencies through a study of geography. The subject is just the medium to develop life skills.
Radical	Change the world. Geography is the way in which pupils can explore social justice issues and gain the knowledge and understanding with which to become activists.
Vocational	Give pupils the skills they will need for the world of work and the knowledge of how geography may make them more employable in the future.

Once you have all identified your own tradition, see if you can reach an agreement as a department as to what you feel the purpose of your curriculum should be. You might also want to consider the capabilities you are hoping to enable in your pupils. What functionings should they have as a result of studying geography with you? Make a list.

Step 2: evaluate

The next step is to look at your current curriculum in light of what you have identified. To what extent is your stated purpose being fulfilled at present? How are the capabilities being developed? Are there any topics that don't fit into your stated purpose? Do they need to be removed completely or just altered? If you are keeping them, why? What other function do they serve?

If you are expected to follow the national curriculum or need to follow an exam specification, then you could also evaluate your curriculum against these documents. It might be useful to check that you are covering all that you need to whilst ensuring that you aren't simply ticking off prescribed content. Have you turned these specifications into an actual curriculum that takes pupils on a journey through our subject?

Step 3: explore the topic

Hopefully, you will now have a list of topics that combine what you currently teach and what you want to teach. The next step is to consider what each topic is going to *do*. What is the propositional and procedural knowledge that you want to develop through studying that topic? What is the fertile question that pupils will be able to answer having studied it? How are the big geographical ideas present in this topic? You can also decide on the places that will be studied in the thematic topics and the themes that you wish to draw upon during the studies of place.

Step 4: sequence

We can now look at sequencing the curriculum. To do this, write out the names of all the topics you wish to teach across the key stage. Pick one at random and ask what your pupils will need to know so that they can access this topic. Then look at the other topics to see where they will have covered this. For example, you have picked "tectonics" and decided that you will answer the fertile question "Are the impacts of volcanic eruptions natural hazards?" Now you realise that pupils will need to have some knowledge of development studies before trying to tackle this, so you know that development studies needs to go before tectonics in your curriculum. You might also decide that the knowledge pupils will gain in the tectonics unit will help them when they come to study geology and landforms and that this, in turn, will be useful when looking at soil and desertification. Now your sequence looks like the diagram on page 169.

Of course, it might not always be so clear-cut. Perhaps you also feel that it would be useful for pupils to have an understanding of soil and desertification when studying development as you want to look at countries in the Sahel region and the barriers to development there. That is a useful reminder that you will need to include some new material on soil in the development topic, which you can then revisit at the start of the soil topic. Over time you should be able to build up a complex web of topics and their connections.

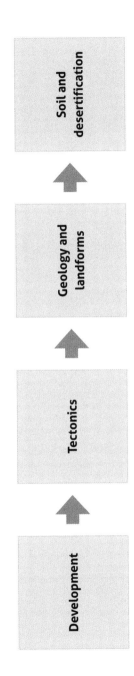

Step 5: plan the pedagogy

Once we have decided on the purpose of our curriculum, the topics we want to teach and the sequence, we can then start to consider the pedagogic tools that will bring it all to life and lead to meaningful learning. This could include:

- The way in which we will identify the key knowledge to be learnt by pupils (those knowledge organisers).

- The way in which we will use retrieval quizzes and hinge questions (questioned asked to check that all pupils have grasped a key point before moving on) in class.

- The role of enquiry, fieldwork and GIS.

- How homework might support the work done in class.

- How we will make the links between topics explicit – through the use of images or questions at the start of lessons.

For more ideas on pedagogy in geography please see *Making Every Geography Lesson Count*.[3]

Step 6: keep it going

A curriculum is a living and breathing thing that exists in the classroom and not on the page. I've already critiqued the empty curriculum intent statement. We might feel comforted by creating a pretty learning map showing the programme of study – we might even have done great work creating the topics and lessons to support it – but if it stays on the page, it dies there. To keep our purposeful curriculum going we need to constantly remind ourselves what we are doing and why. This could take place in department meetings, in which time could be dedicated to discussing upcoming topics, the approaches that teachers will be taking and the rationale behind their decisions.

We also need to ensure that we continue to work on our subject knowledge. When we embrace the potential of powerful knowledge, we have to accept that it gives us nowhere to hide as a teacher. We can't claim that we are all on the learning

3   Enser, *Making Every Geography Lesson Count*.

journey together or that we can succeed if we just stay a page ahead of pupils in the textbook; we have to know our subject inside and out. If we don't, we risk missing the complexities of the discipline. Luckily, as a subject, we are very well served with publications that can help us keep our knowledge up to date. The Geographical Association's *Primary Geography* and *Teaching Geography* (with a focus on secondary) are definitely worth subscribing to, as is the journal *Geography*, which contains articles about the academic discipline and helps us to maintain that link. There are also a wide range of books published every year on geographical topics. The only real difficulty is finding the time to read and share them as a team. If, however, we prioritise the development of subject knowledge, then there is a strong argument that regular CPD time shouldn't be spent daydreaming in a school hall but instead be given over to staff for reading and discussion.

The potential of powerful knowledge

I believe that powerful knowledge has enormous potential to help shape education. It helps to cut through some of the confusion about the purpose of schools by insisting that we focus on those things that other agents in society are not able to provide: the knowledge created by specialist academic disciplines that only experts in both subject knowledge and pedagogy can pass on. It also helps to resolve a centuries-old debate between Future 1 and Future 2 views of knowledge. It accepts the idea that knowledge is contested and can often be subjective (Future 2), but argues that this does not mean we cannot teach this complexity. Likewise, it accepts the idea that there is a body of knowledge to which future generations are entitled (Future 1), but argues that this body of knowledge is always changing and that we should also teach *why* it is changing.

Powerful knowledge also has the potential to fulfil Biesta's ambition of putting the teacher back into education. No more are we facilitators of learning, worried about having to design a curriculum around the fluctuating interests and whims of our pupils. Instead we can joyfully take our place at the front of the classroom and take our pupils on a transformative journey through the subject that we love. We can explore the world with them as we pass on this knowledge as a gift, with the hope that they will use the capabilities they develop to improve the world for the generation that follows them. If we can achieve this, we will have found a new, and powerful, sense of purpose.

Appendix

Notes

The aim of this planning sheet is to give departments opportunities to reflect on their schemes of work and to ensure that all members of the department have the same idea about the intent behind a particular topic and how this intent should be implemented.

It encourages teachers to consider where a topic fits into the bigger picture of their programme of study, what key knowledge and skills pupils are expected to develop and retain, and how this will be assessed. It also asks that we give some thought to the use of homework and further reading.

Prompts

Intent: What is this topic for? Why should it be studied and why should it be studied in this way?

Substantive knowledge: What should pupils know and understand by the end of this topic? What would you expect them to remember about this topic in a year's time?

Procedural knowledge: What should pupils be able to do by the end of this topic? What should they still be able to do in a year's time?

Sequencing: How does one lesson build on another? Why are things taught in this order? How will pupils build on what they have done in previous topics and how will they use this topic in the future?

Threshold concepts: What are the common barriers to pupils understanding this topic? What do they need to know to make sense of this topic?

Misconceptions: What are pupils often mistaken about in this topic? What misconceptions will need drawing out and addressing?

Hinge questions: These are questions asked at key points in a topic to ensure that pupils have understood the threshold concepts and overcome any misconceptions. They are usually best asked as multiple-choice questions in which all the options would seem equally likely to someone who hasn't studied the topic.

Vocabulary: What tier 2 (technical but not subject-specific vocabulary) and tier 3 (subject-specific vocabulary) language will pupils be exposed to in this topic?

Assessment: What formative assessment will be used to ensure that pupils have learnt what you intended them to learn? Most importantly, what plans have you got to address any problems that this assessment reveals?

Homework: How could you use homework to support what is learnt in this topic either by giving chances for deliberate practice or to help pupils review previous learning?

Reading: What could teachers and pupils read to further their understanding of this topic?

Department planning sheet

Topic:

The intent of this topic is that ...

Key propositional knowledge:

Key procedural knowledge/skills:

Sequencing – opportunities for review of previous learning

Lesson sequence:

Links to previous topics:

Links to future topics:

Threshold concepts:

Common misconceptions:

Hinge questions:

1.

2.

3.

Tier 2 vocabulary:

Tier 3 vocabulary:

How will we assess pupil knowledge/understanding/skills during this topic?

How will we respond to any mistakes or misunderstandings that this assessment reveals?

How will homework be used during this topic?

Potential student reading:

Potential teacher reading:

Bibliography

Abel, Magdalena and Henry L. Roediger III (2018) The testing effect in a social setting: does retrieval practice benefit a listener?, *Journal of Experimental Psychology: Applied* 24(3): 347–359.

Adichie, Chimamanda Ngozi (2009) The danger of a single story [video], *TedGlobal* (July). Available at: https://www.ted.com/talks/chimamanda_ngozi_adichie_the_danger_of_a_single_story.

AQA (2016) *GCSE Geography (8035): Specification for Teaching from September 2016 Onward for Exams in 2018 Onwards*. Available at: https://filestore.aqa.org.uk/resources/geography/specifications/AQA-8035-SP-2016.PDF.

ATL (2012) *Report: The Magazine from the Association of Teachers and Lecturers* (May). Available at: https://issuu.com/atlunion/docs/report-may-2012.

Biddulph, Mary (2011) Editorial: "the danger of a single story", *Teaching Geography* 36(2): 45.

Biddulph, Mary (2014) What kind of curriculum do we really want?, *Teaching Geography* 39(1): 6–9.

Biddulph, Mary (2017) What do we mean by curriculum? In Mark Jones (ed.), *The Handbook of Secondary Geography* (Sheffield: The Geographical Association), pp. 30–39.

Biddulph, Mary (2018) Curriculum enactment. In Mark Jones and David Lambert (eds), *Debates in Geography Education*, 2nd edn (Abingdon and New York: Routledge), pp. 156–170.

Biesta, Gert (2013) Receiving the gift of teaching: from "learning from" to "being taught by", *Studies in Philosophy and Education* 32(5): 449–461.

Biesta, Gert (2015) What is education for? On good education, teacher judgement, and educational professionalism, *European Journal of Education* 50(1): 75–87.

Board of Education (1904) *Regulations for Secondary Schools*. Available at: http://www.educationengland.org.uk/documents/boardofed/1904-secondary-regulations.html.

Board of Education (1927) *Report of the Consultative Committee on the Education of the Adolescent* [The 1926 Hadow Report] (London: His Majesty's Stationery Office). Available at: http://www.educationengland.org.uk/documents/hadow1926/hadow1926.html.

Brooks, Clare (2006) Geography teachers and making the school geography curriculum, *Geography* 91(1): 75–83.

Brooks, Clare (2018) Understanding conceptual development in school geography. In Mark Jones and David Lambert (eds), *Debates in Geography Education*, 2nd edn (Abingdon and New York: Routledge), pp. 103–114.

Bruner, Jerome S. (1966) *Toward a Theory of Instruction* (Cambridge, MA: Belknap Press).

Bruner, Jerome (2002) Tenets to understand a cultural perspective on learning. In Bob Moon, Ann Shelton Mayes and Steven Hutchinson (eds), *Teaching, Learning and Curriculum in Secondary Schools: A Reader* (Abingdon and New York: RoutledgeFalmer), pp. 10–24.

Bustin, Richard (2019) *Geography Education's Potential and the Capabilities Approach: GeoCapabilities and Schools* (Cham: Palgrave Macmillan).

Butt, Graham and Gemma Collins (2018) Understanding the gap between schools and universities. In Mark Jones and David Lambert (eds), *Debates in Geography Education*, 2nd edn (Abingdon and New York: Routledge), pp. 263–274.

Catling, Simon and Fran Martin (2011) Contesting powerful knowledge: the primary geography curriculum as an articulation between academic and children's (ethno-) geographies, *The Curriculum Journal* 22(3): 317–335.

Christodoulou, Daisy (2014) *Seven Myths About Education* (Abingdon and New York: Routledge).

Clifford, Nicholas and Alex Standish (2017) Physical geography. In Mark Jones (ed.), *Handbook of Secondary Geography* (Sheffield: The Geographical Association), pp. 62–75.

Cresswell, Tim (2015) *Place: An Introduction*, 2nd edn (Chichester: Wiley Blackwell).

Department for Children, Schools and Families and Qualifications and Curriculum Authority (2007) *The National Curriculum: Statutory Requirements for Key Stages 3 and 4* (London: Department for Children, Schools and Families and Qualifications and Curriculum Authority).

Department for Education (2013) National curriculum in England: geography programmes of study (11 September). Available at: https://www.gov.uk/government/publications/national-curriculum-in-england-geography-programmes-of-study/national-curriculum-in-england-geography-programmes-of-study.

Department for Education (2014) *Geography: GCSE Subject Content*. Ref: DFE-00345-2014. Available at: https://assets.publishing.service.gov.uk/government/uploads/system/uploads/attachment_data/file/301253/GCSE_geography.pdf.

Department of Education and Science (1978) *Primary Education in England: A Survey by HM Inspectors of Schools* (London: Her Majesty's Stationery Office). Available at: http://www.educationengland.org.uk/documents/hmi primary/.

Ebbinghaus, Hermann (1913 [1885]) *Memory: A Contribution to Experimental Psychology*, trs Henry A. Ruger and Clara E. Bussenius (New York: Teachers College, Columbia University).

Egan, John (2004) *The Egan Review: Skills for Sustainable Communities* (London: Office of the Deputy Prime Minister). Available at: https://www.ihbc.org.uk/recent_papers/docs/Egan%20Review%20Skills%20for%20sustainable%20Communities.pdf.

Egan, Kieran (2002) *Getting It Wrong from the Beginning: Our Progressivist Inheritance from Herbert Spencer, John Dewey, and Jean Piaget* (New Haven, CT: Yale University Press).

Enser, Mark (2018) *Making Every Geography Lesson Count: Six Principles to Support Great Geography Teaching* (Carmarthen: Crown House Publishing).

Enser, Mark (2019) Education myths: an origin story. In Craig Barton (ed.), *The researchED Guide to Education Myths: An Evidence-Informed Guide for Teachers* (Woodbridge: John Catt Educational), pp. 19–28.

Fargher, Mary (2017) GIS and other geospatial technologies. In Mark Jones (ed.), *The Handbook of Secondary Geography* (Sheffield: The Geographical Association), pp. 244–259.

Fargher, Mary (2018) Using Geographic Information (GI). In Mark Jones and David Lambert (eds), *Debates in Geography Education*, 2nd edn (Abingdon and New York: Routledge), pp. 197–223.

Ferretti, Jane (2018) The enquiry approach in geography. In Mark Jones and David Lambert (eds), *Debates in Geography Education*, 2nd edn (Routledge: Abingdon and New York), pp. 115–126.

Frean, Alexandra (2008) Google generation has no need for rote learning, *The Times* (2 December).

Freeman, Denise and Alun Morgan (2017) Place and locational knowledge. In Mark Jones (ed.), *Handbook of Secondary Geography* (Sheffield: The Geographical Association), pp. 120–133.

Garner, Richard (2014) What is "the Blob" and why is Michael Gove comparing his enemies to an unbeatable sci-fi mound of goo which once battled Steve McQueen?, *The Independent* (7 February). Available at: https://www.independent.co.uk/news/education/education-news/what-is-the-blob-and-why-is-michael-gove-comparing-his-enemies-to-an-unbeatable-sci-fi-mound-of-goo-9115600.html.

Goudie, Andrew (1993) Schools and universities – the great divide, *Geography* 78(4): 338–339.

Harpaz, Yoram (2005) Teaching and learning in a community of thinking, *Journal of Curriculum and Supervision* 20(2): 136–157.

Heppell, Stephen (2015) Schools of the future must adjust to technological needs, *The Sydney Morning Herald* (16 February). Available at: https://www.smh.com.au/opinion/schools-of-the-future-must-adjust-to-technology-needs-20150216-13fpj9.html.

Hirsch, Jr, E. D. (2016) *Why Knowledge Matters: Rescuing Our Children from Failed Educational Theories* (Cambridge, MA: Harvard University Press).

Holloway, Sarah, Stephen Rice and Gill Valentine (eds) (2003) *Key Concepts in Geography*, 1st edn (London: Sage).

Holt, Latasha (2020) John Dewey: a look at his contributions to curriculum, *Academicus International Scientific Journal* 21: 142–150.

Hopkin, John (2011) Sampling the world, *Teaching Geography* 36(3): 96–97.

Hopkin, John (2015) A "knowledgeable geography" approach to global learning, *Teaching Geography* 40(2): 50–54.

Hopkin, John and Fran Martin (2018) Geography in the National Curriculum for Key Stages 1, 2 and 3. In Mark Jones and David Lambert (eds), *Debates in Geography Education*, 2nd edn (Abingdon and New York: Routledge), pp. 17–32.

Jackson, Peter (2006) Thinking geographically, *Geography* 91(3): 199–204.

Jackson, Peter (2017) Human geography. In Mark Jones (ed.), *Handbook of Secondary Geography* (Sheffield: The Geographical Association), pp. 76–91.

Karpicke, Jeffrey D. and Phillip J. Grimaldi (2012) Retrieval-based learning: a perspective for enhancing meaningful learning, *Educational Psychology Review* 24(3): 401–418.

Kilpatrick, William Heard (1971) *Education for a Changing Civilization: Three Lectures Delivered on the Luther Kellogg Foundation at Rutgers University, 1926* (New York: Arno Press and the New York Times).

Kirschner, Paul A. and Carl Hendrick (2020) *How Learning Happens: Seminal Works in Educational Psychology and What They Mean in Practice* (Abingdon and New York: Routledge).

Kirschner, Paul A., John Sweller and Richard E. Clark (2006) Why minimal guidance during instruction does not work: an analysis of the failure of constructivist, discovery, project-based, experiential, and inquiry-based teaching, *Educational Psychologist* 41(2): 75–86.

Kolb, David A. (1983) *Experiential Learning: Experience as the Source of Learning and Development* (Upper Saddle River, NJ: Prentice Hall).

Lambert, David (2004) The Power of Geography. Available at: https://www.geography.org.uk/write/MediaUploads/Advocacy%20Files/NPOGPower.doc.

Lambert, David (2014) Curriculum thinking, "capabilities" and the place of geographical knowledge in schools, *Journal of Educational Research on Social Studies* 81: 1–11.

Lambert, David (2017) Thinking geographically. In Mark Jones (ed.), *The Handbook of Secondary Geography* (Sheffield: The Geographical Association), pp. 20–29.

Lambert, David and John Morgan (2010) *Teaching Geography 11–18: A Conceptual Approach* (Maidenhead: Open University Press).

Lambert, David, Michael Solem and Sirpa Tani (2015) Achieving human potential through geography education: a capabilities approach to curriculum making in schools, *Annals of the Association of American Geographers* 105(4): 723–735.

Leach, Jenny and Bob Moon (2008) *The Power of Pedagogy* (London: Sage).

Leat, David (2000) The importance of "big" concepts and skills in learning geography. In Chris Fisher and Tony Binns (eds), *Issues in Geography Teaching* (London and New York: RoutledgeFalmer), pp. 137–151.

Leat, David (ed.) (2017) *Enquiry and Project Based Learning: Students, School and Society* (Abingdon and New York: Routledge).

Mackinder, Halford (1887) On the scope and methods of geography, *Proceedings of the Royal Geographical Society and Monthly Record of Geography* 9(3): 141–174.

Marsden, Bill (1997) On taking the geography out of geographical education: some historical pointers, *Geography* 82(3): 241–252.

Martin, Fran (2008) Ethnogeography: towards liberatory geography education, *Children's Geographies* 6(4): 437–450.

Martin, Fran (2013) The place of knowledge in the new curriculum, *Primary Geography* 82(3): 9–11.

Maude, Alaric (2016) What might powerful geographical knowledge look like?, *Geography* 101(2): 70–76.

Meyer, Jan H. F. and Ray Land (2003) Threshold concepts and troublesome knowledge: linkages to ways of thinking and practising within the disciplines. In Chris Rust (ed.), *Improving Student Learning: Theory and Practice Ten Years On* (Oxford: Oxford Centre for Staff and Learning Development), pp. 412–424.

Morgan, John and David Lambert (2005) *Geography: Teaching School Subjects 11–19* (Abingdon and New York: Routledge).

Nussbaum, Martha C. (2000) *Women and Human Development: The Capabilities Approach* (Cambridge: Cambridge University Press).

OCR (2019) OCR A Level Geography H481/04/05 Investigative Geography Mark Recording Sheet. Available at: https://www.ocr.org.uk/Images/349152-a-level-mark-recording-sheet.pdf.

Peal, Robert (2014) *Progressively Worse: The Burden of Bad Ideas in British Schools* (London: Civitas).

Puttick, Steve (2020) Raising issues: taking Burgess out of the bin, *Teaching Geography* 45(1): 6–8.

Rawding, Charles (2013) Challenging assumptions: the importance of holistic geographies, *Geography* 98(3): 157–159.

Rawding, Charles (2018) The Anthropocene and the global. In Mark Jones and David Lambert (eds), *Debates in Geography Education*, 2nd edn (Abingdon and New York: Routledge), pp. 240–249.

Rawding, Charles (2019) Raising issues: putting Burgess in the bin, *Teaching Geography* 44(3): 94–96.

Rawling, Eleanor (2000) Ideology, politics and curriculum change: reflections on school geography 2000, *Geography* 85(3): 209–220.

Rawling, Eleanor (2018) Place in geography: change and challenge. In Mark Jones and David Lambert (eds), *Debates in Geography Education*, 2nd edn (Abingdon and New York: Routledge), pp. 49–61.

Rawling, Eleanor (2020) How and why national curriculum frameworks are failing geography, *Geography* 105(2): 69–77.

Rayner, David (2017) Resources. In Mark Jones (ed.), *The Handbook of Secondary Geography* (Sheffield: The Geographical Association), pp. 150–165.

Rickinson, Mark, Justin Dillon, Kelly Teamey, Marian Morris, Mee Young Choi, Dawn Sanders and Pauline Benefield (2014) *A Review of Research on Outdoor Learning* (Slough: National Foundation for Education Research and King's College London).

Roberts, Margaret (2003) *Learning Through Enquiry: Making Sense of Geography in the Key Stage 3 Classroom* (Sheffield: The Geographical Association).

Roberts, Margaret (2013) *Geography Through Enquiry: Approaches to Teaching and Learning in the Secondary School* (Sheffield: The Geographical Association).

Roberts, Margaret (2014) Powerful knowledge and geographical education, *The Curriculum Journal* 25(2): 187–209.

Robeyns, Ingrid (2006) Three models of education: rights, capabilities and human capital, *Theory and Research in Education* 4(1): 69–84.

Rosenshine, Barak (2012) Principles of instruction: research-based strategies that all teachers should know, *American Educator* 36(1): 12–19, 39. Available at: https://www.aft.org/sites/default/files/ periodicals/Rosenshine.pdf.

Rousseau, Jean-Jacques (1911 [1762]) *Émile, Or On Education*, tr. Barbara Foxley (London: Dent).

Sealy, Clare (2019) Memorable experiences are the best way to help children remember things. In Craig Barton (ed.), *The researchED Guide to Education Myths: An Evidence-Informed Guide for Teachers* (Woodbridge: John Catt Educational), pp. 29–40.

Sen, Amartya (1989) Development as capability expansion, *Journal of Development Planning* 19: 41–58.

Sfard, Anna (1998) On two metaphors for learning and the dangers of choosing just one, *Educational Researcher* 27(2): 4–13.

Solem, Michael, David Lambert and Sirpa Tani (2013) Geocapabilities: toward an international framework for researching the purposes and values of geography education, *Review of International Geographical Education* 3(3): 214–229. Available at: http://www.rigeo.org/vol3no3/RIGEO-V3-N3-1.pdf.

Standish, Alex (2003) Constructing a value map, *Geography* 88(2): 149–151.

Standish, Alex (2004) Valuing (adult) geographic knowledge, *Geography* 89(1): 89–91.

Standish, Alex (2009) *Global Perspectives in the Geography Curriculum: Reviewing the Moral Case for Geography* (Abingdon and New York: Routledge).

Standish, Alex (2017) Geography. In Alex Standish and Alka Sehgal Cuthbert (eds), *What Should Schools Teach? Disciplines, Subjects and the Pursuit of Truth* (London: UCL Institute of Education Press), pp. 88–103.

Standish, Alex (2018) The place of regional geography. In Mark Jones and David Lambert (eds), *Debates in Geography Education*, 2nd edn (Abingdon and New York: Routledge), pp. 62–74.

Standish, Alex and Alka Sehgal Cuthbert (eds) (2017) *What Should Schools Teach? Disciplines, Subjects and the Pursuit of Truth* (London: UCL Institute of Education Press).

Tate, Nicholas (2015) *What Is Education For? The View of the Great Thinkers and Their Relevance Today* (Woodbridge: John Catt Educational).

Taylor, Liz (2005) Place: an exploration, *Teaching Geography* 30(1): 14–17.

Taylor, Liz (2008) Key concepts and medium term planning, *Teaching Geography* 33(2): 50–54.

Taylor, Liz (2017) Progression. In Mark Jones (ed.), *The Handbook of Secondary Geography* (Sheffield: The Geographical Association), pp. 40–47.

Wadley, David A. (2008) The garden of peace, *Annals of the Association of American Geographers* 98(3): 650–685.

Warwick, Paul (2016) Education for Sustainable Development: a movement towards pedagogies of civic compassion, *Forum* 58(3): 407–414.

Widdowson, John and Alan Parkinson (2013) *Fieldwork Through Enquiry* (Sheffield: The Geographical Association).

Young, Michael (2008) *Bringing Knowledge Back In: From Social Constructivism to Social Realism in the Sociology of Education* (Abingdon and New York: Routledge).

Young, Michael and David Lambert (2014) *Knowledge and the Future School: Curriculum and Social Justice* (London: Bloomsbury).

Young, Michael and Johan Muller (2010) Three educational scenarios for the future: lessons for the sociology of knowledge, *European Journal of Education* 45(1): 11–27.